D0885264

The Romanovs

An Enthralling Overview of the House of Romanov

Free limited time bonus

Stop for a moment. We have a free bonus set up for you. The problem is this: we forget 90% of everything that we read after 7 days. Crazy fact, right? Here's the solution: we've created a printable, 1-page pdf summary for this book that you're reading now. All you have to do to get your free pdf summary is to go to the following website:

https://livetolearn.lpages.co/enthrallinghistory/

Once you do, it will be intuitive. Enjoy, and thank you!

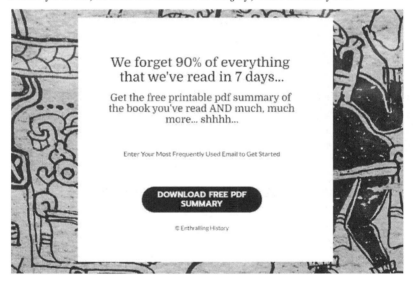

Table of Contents

Introduction

When it comes to listing the most iconic or infamous dynasties throughout world history, several names instantly come to mind. Powerful families have always challenged each other for dominance in different parts of the world—something that largely characterized the social and political landscapes of ancient, medieval, and early modern times. These families often emerged from the uncertain and chaotic political turmoil of their respective regions and time periods as superior rulers, forming dynasties, some of which would last for centuries. For example, in the competitive societies of ancient China and Japan, dynasties temporarily rose to power and united their dominions, defining entire eras and playing important roles in the establishment of distinct cultural, social, and political characteristics. The Meiji Restoration period of 19th-century Japan under the Meiji dynasty is rather notable, while the Ming and Qing dynasties dominated China beginning in the early 14th century.

Unlike medieval Asia, where a single dynasty often overpowered the others to enjoy a period of solitary rule, powerful European dynasties often existed simultaneously in different countries, something that can only be attributed to the cultural and ethnic diversity present in the continent. Some of these European family names, like the Habsburgs and the Bourbons, are recognizable even to the most casual of history enthusiasts. Thriving in competition with each other and remaining at the top for centuries, the European dynasties are well known for their roles in history and have been a subject of fascination because of the complexities that characterized them.

However, when it comes to the famous dynasties of Europe, perhaps none are as intriguing as the Romanov dynasty, a family that ruled Russia for around three hundred years. Their renown stems from the fact that Russia itself, as a sovereign nation-state, has had an interesting journey, with the country undergoing the most substantial and long-lasting transformations of any European superpower. The different state-like formations in Russia struggled for centuries to find their true identity, plagued by their difficult, remote geographical location at the meeting point of European and Asian cultures and constantly bothered by either external threats or domestic instabilities.

Although the Rurikid dynasty can be considered the most powerful in Russian history (after all, the legendary Rurik was the one to organize the primitive settlements in the area as a Russian proto-state, and his descendants generally ruled the different provinces in the centuries that followed), the socio-political structures in place would make it rather difficult for a single family to emerge on top of the hierarchy and keep their position of power. Instead, the history of medieval Russia is filled with instances of dominant rulers who would leave their mark due to their explosive, charismatic personalities, although there was a plethora of forgettable ones. The combination of all the above-mentioned facts makes the Romanov dynasty stand out even more, as it is truly fascinating how a single family maintained its firm rule over so many of its subjects in such a chaotic place.

Thus, this book will explore the history of the Romanovs—Russia's greatest dynasty—from its relatively humble beginnings to the height of its power to its rather brutal end. First, the book will dive deep into the background before the emergence of the Romanovs. The first chapters will be concerned with the final days of the Rurikids and the Time of Troubles, a period in Russian history where uncertainty and chaos reigned. We will then talk about the first Romanovs, who slowly managed to unify the vast and unruly Russian provinces and provide a basis for a little over three centuries of firm rule. Next, the book will explore the consolidation of the dynasty under the enlightened despotism of Catherine the Great, as well as the challenges the Romanovs had to face during the early 19th century against Napoleon.

The middle part of the book discusses the rest of the Romanov rulers. We cover their most notable contributions to Russia and the rest of Europe up until the start of World War I. Finally, the book will talk about the rather difficult parts of the Romanov rule in the early 20th century, including the country's involvement in the Great War, the Bolshevik Revolution, and the tragic end of the Russian monarchy.

Chapter One – Before the Romanovs

Before we discuss the Romanov dynasty, we should first briefly look at the two hundred years or so before the Romanovs came to power. As a matter of fact, the 14th and 15th centuries were vital for Russia since "Russia," as the state we know today, would form during this period. Therefore, it is only logical to go over those social and political developments in the 1300s and 1400s that stimulated the unification of many different principalities and explain how they affected the course of Russian history. This first chapter of the book will be concerned with covering the very interesting period immediately before the first true Russian state, discussing the emergence of Moscow (also known as Muscovy) as a new center for Russian civilization and the immense implications it had on the geopolitical climate.

Briefly on Medieval Russia

It is important to mention that Russia, as a unified state, was still a new phenomenon in the mid-16th century. Throughout history, the rulers of Russia, known as the grand princes, faced a lot of difficulties because of the decentralization of power that was innate in the political landscape, which was diverse and thinly stretched out. Many larger and smaller provinces were ruled by individual princes, who, in theory, were loyal to the grand prince but, in practice, acted as independently as they desired. They were in all aspects "Russian," as they spoke the same language, pursued the same culture and religion, and came from the same descendants. But the complex power politics that characterized the dynamic relationships between them made it so they never lived in harmony, coexisting instead as rivals, ready to rise to the top as soon as they saw the opportunity. This had been the case for hundreds of years, ever since the legendary Rurik had come down from Scandinavia to unite the primitive settlements in the Russian territories under his rule. His descendants—the Rurikids—had since ruled the Russian people, with some of them certainly finding better success than others.

The lands ruled by the Rurikid princes and their subordinates were referred to by other Europeans as "the lands of the Rus" for about five hundred or so years after the death of Rurik, although "Russia" as a unified state would take much longer to emerge. Challenged by the interests of individual princes and constant foreign threats, including the nearly two-and-a-half centuries of Mongol occupation, the Russian rulers had to struggle for their own survival before they could try uniting their subordinates and forming a strong state. Because of the difficult circumstances, Russia eventually fell behind to Europe. Russia was influenced by several different ideologies and struggled to find its own identity for centuries, something that would later be heavily addressed by the likes of Peter the Great.

These circumstances also influenced another phenomenon, which would repeat itself throughout not only the medieval times but also during the reign of the Romanovs: in order to have at least some hope of effectively resisting the challenges that presented themselves over and over again, the Russian people needed a strong leader, someone capable of uniting the rival princes and reforming the country from top to bottom. In different centuries, several individuals scratched the surface of this, emerging as powerful leaders who led the Russian people for a short period of greatness, only for the country to experience a rapid period of decline after their death. This was perhaps the biggest problem medieval Russia faced. Although some kings and princes managed to briefly lead the Russians to stability, they were rarely able to organize a strong basis for their successors to continue on the same trajectory.

The Grand Duchy of Muscovy

Russia existed in this state of struggle for several centuries, all while different princes from different provinces temporarily rose to the top and replaced each other. From the fall of Kievan Rus', the "first" strong Russian state, to the rise of the Mongols in the 13th century, several different Russian principalities challenged each other for dominance. The city of Kiev (also spelled as Kyiv), once the most prosperous in all of Eastern Europe after Constantinople itself, was ravaged not only by the Mongol horde but also by Russians who were eager to see the Rus' fall. The title of the grand prince was assumed by the ruler of Vladimir, a city in the far northeastern province of Vladimir-Suzdal, and the center of Russian civilization shifted from the lands near the Dnieper River all the way to the Volga River and its surrounding principalities. During the Mongol occupation, Vladimir-Suzdal remained the most important Russian principality, becoming a favorite of the khanate but, nevertheless, failing to spread its influence to the rest of the Russian lands.

Novgorod was another powerful principality in Russia. It was located in the northwestern part of the country and controlled a vast territory in northern Russia, including parts of the Baltic Sea. Due to Novgorod's great geographical location, it had always been one of the richest and most prosperous principalities, but unlike its rivals, it was hardly ever interested in dominating the rest of the Russian lands. In a way, Novgorodians always had a sense of superiority, opting to limit their involvement in Russian politics unless absolutely necessary or unless it would grant them direct benefits. From the 12th to the 15th century, Novgorod existed as a separate republic, the first of its kind in Russia. It was effectively ruled by a democratic city council.

Vladimir-Suzdal and Novgorod were only two of the big Russian principalities. The others, like the central cities of Chernigov (today's Chernihiv) and Smolensk, Ryazan in the east, or Polotsk at the Polish-Lithuanian border in the west, were also important actors in Russian politics, but none of them managed to gain a significant edge over the others. Eventually, a rather unlikely contestant claimed the title of the most powerful Russian province.

In an interesting turn of events, by the early 14th century, a small, relatively unimportant town by the name of Moscow, located at the southern border of Vladimir-Suzdal, started almost exponentially growing its power by gaining control over its bordering territories. Daniil (Daniel) Nevsky, the ruler of Moscow in the early 14th century and the youngest son of the powerful ex-ruler of Vladimir-Suzdal Alexander Nevsky, seized the neighboring territory of Kolomna, allowing him to control the important point where the Moskva River joined with the Volga. His son, Yuri, continued his efforts, quickly imprisoning the prince of Mozhaysk in the west in 1303 and almost doubling his possessions. Still, compared to other principalities, the territory held by Yuri of Moscow was insignificant; however, a good enough base had been established to challenge Moscow's much-larger neighbors for dominance.

It is important to highlight that by this time, the Mongols were still reigning freely in Russia. To assume the title of grand prince, the candidate must pay a visit to the khan and ask for a *yarlyk*—a blessing from the Mongol ruler to become the grand prince of the Russian principalities. He also had to pledge his allegiance to the horde. After imprisoning the prince of Mozhaysk, Prince Yuri visited the khan to try and gain the *yarlyk*, arguing that he had a legitimate claim since he was a descendant of Alexander Nevsky. However, the khan instead gave the *yarlyk* to Mikhail of Tver, the ruler of a neighboring province who had promised the khan more concessions and a larger amount of yearly tribute.

This complicated the relationship between Yuri and Mikhail, and Moscow and Tver soon became fierce rivals. Fortunately for Yuri, Mikhail proved to be an unsuccessful ruler. He not only failed to live up to the khan's expectations but also angered the Orthodox Russians when he tried to install his preferred candidate as the new head of the church in Vladimir. The rightful Metropolitan Peter, the one who had been installed from Constantinople (the Russian Church was not independent by then), had no reason to support Mikhail of Tver, who had effectively tried to reduce his legitimacy by challenging his position. Metropolitan Peter instead forged a close relationship with Yuri of Moscow. His successor, Metropolitan Theognostus, was influenced by his predecessor and later transferred the official seat of the metropolitan of Russia to the city of Moscow, greatly increasing the city's importance in the eyes of the Russian people and starting the chain of events that would eventually lead to Moscow's rise to prominence.

In the following years, Yuri of Moscow managed to wrestle the title of grand prince away from Mikhail of Tver by personally visiting the city of Sarai on the Lower Volga—the seat of the khan of the Golden Horde—and forging close relations with the new khan, Uzbeg. He even managed to marry the khan's sister, Konchaka. After gaining the backing of the horde, Yuri officially managed to secure the khan's *yarlyk*, earning him the title of grand prince. It was pivotal, as Yuri was now not only the prince of Moscow but also the grand prince of Vladimir-Suzdal, the de-facto capital of medieval Russia, earning him much-needed fame and status.

For the rest of the 14th century, the principality of Muscovy tried to expand its influence over the bordering territories, although it was constantly challenged by Tver. However, after gaining the horde's favor, Muscovy was in a much more advantageous position. The Muscovite rulers forged alliances with different principalities, and these agreements would come in handy. The city of Moscow started to grow in importance, especially thanks to the seat of the metropolitan being transferred to it. Eventually, after the fall of Constantinople in 1453, Moscow would famously claim the title of "Third Rome," further stressing its status not only in Russia but also in all of the Christian world.

Ivan Kalita, the younger brother of Yuri who gained the nickname Kalita ("moneybag") because of his generous nature, would further consolidate and expand the power held by Muscovy. Ivan Kalita acquired new territories in the Transvolga, bringing Muscovy closer to the Asian trade routes, which ensured the flow of new riches into his realm. Crucially, during his reign, the title of grand prince started to be taken more seriously by the princes.

Thanks to Ivan Kalita's territorial acquisitions, he was in charge of a very large piece of land and had the ambition to consider himself not only the grand prince of Vladimir-Suzdal but also of all of Russia. This distinction would soon start to take shape, as the grand prince would begin to be the only person allowed to have direct contact with the khan. Before, any prince could approach the ruler of the horde in cases of necessity.

As Muscovy's influence grew, so did the number of its enemies. At the time of Ivan Kalita's death in 1340, almost all of the eastern Russian principalities had been virtually united, having sworn loyalty to the grand prince in Vladimir. This consolidation of power in the east, in turn, caused the western principalities to fall prey to the neighboring Kingdom of Lithuania, whose Grand Prince Olgerd managed to gain control of most of western Russia by the 1350s and even seized Kiev in 1361. Olgerd saw Muscovy as his direct rival and a threat to Catholic Lithuania, so he journeyed out to capture the city on three different occasions but was ultimately unsuccessful.

In 1375, Olgerd sought help from Prince Mikhail Aleksandrovich of Tver, who had secretly negotiated the *yarlyk* with the khan in Sarai. Together, the two marched against the city of Vladimir, with Mikhail claiming to be the new grand prince, but both of them were eventually driven back by Grand Prince Dmitry Donskoy of Moscow and Vladimir-Suzdal. Dmitry's army consisted mostly of troops from the regions that had been acquired during Muscovy's expansion, further stressing the fact these principalities were loyal to the grand prince.

After learning the Mongols had negotiated with Mikhail of Tver behind Grand Prince Dmitry's back, the relationship between the Golden Horde and Muscovy started to slowly deteriorate. Technically, the Muscovite rulers still needed *yarlyks* from Sarai to be named grand prince, but as we already mentioned, the position had largely become independent from the Mongols and gained much more prominence after Moscow's rise. In addition, the Golden Horde was facing countless internal issues, with different clans, descendants of the great Genghis Khan, squabbling with each over the control of the empire's vast lands.

By the late 1370s, the Mongols would regularly attack and raid the lands ruled by Muscovy, something that caused doubts in the minds of Muscovite officials on whether or not the Mongol rule was beneficial for the country's future. Crucially, in 1380, in another attempt to undermine the growing power of Moscow, the Mongol leader, Mamai Khan, led a force of about 200,000 men against Prince Dmitry, the latter of whom was supported by the prince of Ryazan and the Lithuanians. Grand Prince Dmitry met the enemy at Kulikovo near the River Don with about 150,000 soldiers and was able to decisively defeat the Mongols. This legendary victory earned Dmitry his nickname "Donskoy" ("of the Don"). The Battle of Kulikovo would be the first sign of Russian resistance against Mongol rule. The Mongols would eventually be driven out of Russia about one hundred years later.

Ivan the Great

Despite the success at Kulikovo, the Mongol rulers were adamant about keeping their influence over the leaders of Russia and proceeded to retaliate by quickly mustering up new armies to attack Muscovy while Dmitry Donskoy was recovering from his losses. In the early 1380s, Mongol cavalry raids devastated the countryside of the Lower Volga, with Russian settlements falling prey to the invaders and causing an economic recession that slowed down Muscovite expansion. However, these incursions did not break Muscovy's unity, and Dmitry Donskoy's son and successor, Vasily I, managed to hold onto the expanded territories. Instead of answering the Mongols with more aggression, Vasily I adopted a peaceful approach, visiting Sarai and asking the new khan for his forgiveness and blessing. He knew that despite all the success Muscovy had had over the past decades that it was still too early to engage in an all-out war for liberation. In addition, Vasily I consolidated the power Moscow held over the neighboring princes and further contributed to forming the basis of what would later become Russia, knowing that liberation from Mongol rule was close at hand. The Russians just needed to patiently wait for the opportunity to strike.

The Muscovite ruler that would eventually lead the Russians to independence was Vasily I's grandson, Ivan III, now known as "the Great" for his efforts. Ascending to the throne in 1462, Ivan III found himself in the middle of a complex political climate. Among the latest geopolitical developments was the fall of Constantinople to the Ottomans in 1453, which amplified the symbolic role of Moscow as the "Third Rome" and the new torchbearer for all of Christianity. In addition, his father, Vasily II, had struggled with neighboring Prince Yuri of Galich for dominance over the Russian lands, as well as with the Lithuanians, who had increased their influence over the western Russian principalities. Crucially, however, the most interesting occurrence was undoubtedly the further weakening of the Mongol Empire and its division into multiple rivaling realms. There was the Crimean Khanate, which occupied the northern coast of the Black Sea, and there was the Kazan Khanate in the east. This split complicated the power dynamics of the region and especially affected the Russian rulers, who were confused as to which khanate was more legitimate. It was apparent that the Mongols, in one way or another, were losing their control of Russia.

Ivan the Great realized that he needed to act. He first started to consolidate his power by forging close ties with the boyar nobility, who were the main landowners and catalysts in the Muscovite armies. He implemented new etiquette rules to boost the significance of the title of grand prince and made sure that all the lesser princes strictly followed them. Ivan was the first ruler to adopt the title of tsar, which was adopted from the Roman word Caesar.

A very impactful decision Ivan III made was to wage a campaign against Novgorod in 1471, during which he managed to finally subjugate the rich city and its lands after centuries of being free. Being in control of Novgorod had, in the past, proven to be crucial for gaining any sort of military or economic advantage for Russian rulers, and Ivan III was no exception. He installed a Muscovite governor in the city and limited its freedom and local governance before eventually incorporating it into the territories of Muscovy. Ivan also defeated the long-standing rival principalities of Tver and Ryazan, taking firm control over their lands and leading Muscovy to the most dominant position it had ever enjoyed.

Then came the main objective of liberation from the Mongols. Recognizing the hostile relationship between the different khanates, Ivan the Great assembled his army, with different principalities contributing troops from their lands, and forged an alliance with the Crimean Khanate to make a stand against Sarai and the remainder of the Golden Horde. In 1480, the Great Horde's Ahmed Khan campaigned against Moscow with the same objective as many of his ancestors: to "punish" the overly-confident Russians and reassert Mongol dominance.

In October, the two armies met at the Ugra River, where Ivan had assumed a defensive position. He knew the Mongols, with their famous cavalry, were more favored to win an open battle, so he decided to stall, waiting for winter to arrive, which would force the enemy to retreat. In what has come to be known as the Great Stand at Ugra, the two sides engaged in combat multiple times, with Ahmed Khan and his mighty army trying unsuccessfully to cross the river. After failing time and time again, winter rolled around, and just as Ivan had hoped, the weather forced the Mongols back without them having made any progress.

The Great Stand was a crucial victory for Ivan and Muscovy and is considered to be the end of Mongol rule over Russia. After the invaders went back to Sarai, Ivan never paid them the yearly tribute, and the title of *yarlyk* would never again be bestowed to future rulers. The Great Horde (what was left of the Golden Horde) would soon see its complete demise due to internal squabbles. Ahmed Khan was assassinated by his rivals, and the Great Horde would then be conquered by the Crimean Khanate in the 16th century. Russia was now finally free from the Mongols.

Although the liberation from the Mongols is considered to be Ivan III's greatest achievement, he contributed much to the formation of a stable, unified Russian state. We have already briefly mentioned the domestic policies that allowed him to centralize more power. With Moscow's increased importance as the new center of Christianity, Ivan the Great's reign is considered to be a sort of a renaissance for the Russian Orthodox Church, which was greatly reformed and modernized. The church, for the first time in a long while, transformed from an institution associated strictly with the highest classes to something universal. Monasticism became a noble pursuit, and Orthodoxy occupied a central part in the lives of the Russian people. Respect for religion became infused in the collective minds of the Russians and was arguably one of the first true Russian national identities. New churches were built, and the clergy developed a good relationship with the grand prince, who never hesitated to aid them.

Ivan the Great also shined when it came to foreign policy, becoming the first Russian ruler to forge diplomatic ties with many different European and Middle Eastern states, like the Holy Roman Empire, the Ottoman Empire, and Persia. He also stabilized the situation in the western Russian principalities by making peace with the Livonian Order on the Baltic coast, which he considered a future corridor into the Western world. This concept would be further developed by Peter I when he constructed the first Baltic Russian port of St. Petersburg. In the late 1590s, Ivan III turned his attention to the ever-growing Lithuanian threat in the west, defeating the Lithuanian princes in several encounters and forcing them to renounce their claims on the bordering Russian lands. By the early 16th century, Ivan had successfully undermined Lithuania's position and reached a peace deal.

All in all, Ivan the Great, the first tsar, was undoubtedly one of the most influential leaders of Muscovy. He quickly consolidated his status and power after becoming the grand prince, expanded the realms in his possession, liberated the country from the tyrannical rule of the Mongols, and reformed Moscow's institutions to achieve a period of domestic stability and economic growth. During his reign, Muscovy emerged as a dominant player in the region and experienced great progress toward the formation of the first unified Russian state.

Chapter Two – The Last of the Rurikids

Before the Romanovs took over the rule of Russia and became one of the most famous dynasties in world history, the nation experienced a period of slow decline that eventually resulted in the final days of the Rurikid dynasty. The highs of Ivan the Great would only last for so long before the country descended once again into chaos. After the death of Tsar Ivan IV (Ivan the Terrible, as he has come to be infamously known in history due to a number of atrocities he committed during his reign), Russia found itself in a period of turmoil, despair, and uncertainty. This short but impactful era, fittingly named the "Time of Troubles," was a pivotal point in Russian history and marked the end of both the Rurikids and medieval Russia, acting as a "gateway" to early modern times.

The first Romanovs rose to prominence during the Time of Troubles, so it is natural that the focus of this chapter is on discussing those circumstances in detail to better understand the emergence of the new Russian dynasty.

Succession Difficulties

Despite Ivan the Terrible's rather appropriate nickname, he was, in fact, one of the better kings Russia had seen in a long time when he ascended the throne in 1547. He became tsar after a brief succession crisis that emerged in Muscovy during the final years of Ivan the Great's reign and persisted for decades after his death in 1505. Different sons of Ivan III claimed legitimacy over the Muscovite throne for about forty years, an occurrence caused by the fact the king had children from both of his marriages. The heir to the throne, Ivan the Young, who was the only son of Ivan the Great and his first wife, Maria of Tver, tragically passed in 1490, leaving the old king with a difficult problem of succession. The next decades saw the struggle for succession break out between Vasily, the eldest son of Ivan the Great and his second wife, Sophia Palaiologina, and Dmitry, the son of Ivan the Young. Eventually, the former came out on top and was crowned Vasily III in the first decade of the 16th century.

Vasily III's reign was focused on consolidating the grand prince's power, which had noticeably dwindled away, with some lesser princes being unwilling to bend the knee to the new ruler. However, Muscovy's succession crisis did not stop there, as the new king had no heirs. After obtaining a blessing from Metropolitan Daniel, he divorced his wife Solomonia, forcing her to become a nun, and instead married Yelena (also known as Elena) Glinskaya, who finally bore him a son, Ivan. Three years later, in 1533, Vasily III unexpectedly passed away, making Ivan (now Ivan IV) the grand prince of Muscovy at only three years old, which meant Yelena became a regent before her son came of age.

Throughout her time as the regent, Yelena tried her best to protect the throne from various competitors, who tried to take advantage of the fact the Crown was weak. Among the contenders were Vasily III's brothers, who all believed they had legitimate claims to the throne since they were the sons of Ivan the Great. For the next thirteen years, the brothers instigated numerous rebellions to try and take over the city of Moscow and claimed the title of grand prince on numerous occasions. They might have succeeded in undermining Queen Yelena and the rest of the royal supporters, but they lacked public backing and unity—something that eventually resulted in none of them coming out on top.

Different lesser princes also challenged the young Ivan, but, to the surprise of many, the Crown persevered. Ivan IV finally came of age and was fit enough to rule in 1547. The fact he had retained control over the throne signaled the strong foundation that had been built by Ivan the Great, but it by no means meant Ivan IV's reign would be free of troubles.

Ivan the Terrible

A painting of Ivan the Terrible by Viktor Mikhailovich Vasnetsov.
https://commons.wikimedia.org/wiki/File:Ivan_the_Terrible_(cropped).JPG

Thus, Ivan the Terrible became the new tsar in 1547. Although he was still very young (he was only seventeen years old), he immediately got to work. Ivan was relatively inexperienced compared to his grandfather but did enjoy support from some of the most influential figures in Russia at the time. One of those people was Metropolitan Makary, and the first reforms the new tsar passed concerned nearly all aspects of Russia's religious life. The first three years of Ivan's reign would see two ecclesiastical councils, each led by the metropolitan, that would eventually produce a hundred-chapter statute book by the name of *Stoglav*, which carefully described and regulated religious matters. Among the new reforms was the crucial implementation of a new Russian

Orthodox calendar with dates to commemorate the saints, which, in turn, resulted in the creation of new rest days. The *Stoglav* also touched upon the details regarding worship at religious sites and increased the number of lands the church possessed, a change that was a clear indication that the church had royal support.

In 1551, a new legislative code was introduced in one of the ecclesiastic councils. This new piece of legislation, by the name of Sudebnik, proposed new laws regarding court proceedings and serf and land ownership. New forms of punishment for crimes were also added, greatly expanding the already existing legislation. All in all, Ivan IV's first few years as tsar saw not only an amplification of the Russian Orthodox Church's importance but also legislative expansion to modernize Muscovy.

Throughout the 1550s, Ivan IV tried to centralize the monarchy's power, following in the footsteps of his grandfather. In Moscow, he assembled his own advisory council, which was made up of his most trusted allies. The council informally assisted Ivan in all major decisions. In the provinces, Ivan reduced the power held by the local governors by giving them limited access to local law-making and instead granting them new responsibilities of dealing with crime and corruption. Ivan and his *Izbrannaya Rada* ("chosen council") handpicked administrative representatives from Moscow and placed them in positions of power in the capitals of principalities. These individuals reported directly to the council and worked on implementing the changes the local populations desired the most while being reliant on Moscow in terms of protection. The principalities were also assigned fixed yearly tax rates based on their economic status.

The reform that produced perhaps the best results for Ivan IV's realm was the long-overdue modernization of the military. New laws not only regulated the number of soldiers each landowner had to provide the Crown during wartime but also resulted in the creation of elite military contingents that would be given estates in Moscow and were expected to be ready for service at all times. The army became more disciplined, thanks to the yearly training sessions in Moscow that assured the men's readiness for combat. These changes proved more than effective, as Ivan IV was able to finally put an end to the Kazan Khanate's raids and gradually conquered the territories held by the Mongol realm. In the end, the tsar gained control of virtually all of the Volga River by 1556.

Unfortunately for Ivan IV, the successful early campaigns against the Mongols in the east would not be followed up by similar triumphs elsewhere. Instead of focusing his army to the south to take over the lands held by the Crimean Khanate and gain access to the northern coast of the Black Sea, the ambitious tsar turned his attention to the Baltic, a region whose importance had been greatly amplified by Ivan the Great. When Ivan IV restarted the war against the Livonians in 1558, Muscovy did not have direct access to the Baltic Sea. Although the Livonian Order quickly disintegrated after being repeatedly targeted by bigger powers over the next decades, the war for the Baltic would last for another twenty-four years and would take up much of Muscovy's necessary resources.

By the late 1570s, Ivan IV was constantly at war against the kingdoms of Sweden, Lithuania, and Poland, and despite making initial progress, he was feeling the toll of the war due to domestic and external pressure. The military reform was not enough for Muscovy to put up a fight on multiple fronts against multiple enemies, and in 1582 and 1583, Ivan IV was forced to sign peace treaties, making significant territorial concessions to his enemies.

As the war effort proved increasingly difficult to maintain, Ivan's reign entered a period of decline, and the decisions taken by the tsar would eventually earn him his infamous nickname, "the Terrible." Throughout the 1560s, his actions increased the tsar's power even more and, in many cases, can only be classified as purely authoritarian. In 1564, for example, all Russian territories were divided into *zemshchina* (the state lands) and *oprichnina* (lands in possession of the tsar). The Crown's possessions increased quite dramatically due to this change. The servants of the *oprichnina* were then recruited as a special police force and would basically do anything the tsar desired. These individuals, called *oprichniki*, were used by Tsar Ivan IV to spy on his subjects and enforce his ruthlessness upon them if he suspected anything malicious of them. Although the *oprichniki* apprehended many landowners, boyars, and officeholders, the institution proved to be fatal for the well-being of the tsar, who became increasingly paranoid.

This paranoia and constant search for conspiracies against his rule started because of the unfruitful military campaigns in the Baltic. One by one, Ivan IV started arresting, exiling, or outright murdering those who had been with him since the beginning of his reign. For example, Ivan IV arrested members of his chosen council after they talked him into signing a peace deal with the Livonians in 1560. By 1564, the tsar had grown so arrogant and paranoid that he regarded the victory of his friend, Prince Kurbsky, against the Polish as a threat to the throne. Ivan also suffered a couple of psychological traumas. The passing of his wife, Anastasia, and his closest friend, Metropolitan Makary, induced more stress. Ivan's fears of a conspiratorial boyar rebellion against his rule made him leave Moscow and threaten abdication in time of war in the mid-1560s. During all this time, the *oprichniki* continued to ruthlessly arrest any suspicious person, and it was clear the tsar's personal police force served not to enforce laws but to personally complete the tasks given to them by Ivan.

The unlawfulness and chaos reached their peak when the tsar's cousin, Prince Vladimir, admitted the existence of a boyar conspiracy to overthrow Ivan after being arrested and tortured by the *oprichniki*. This had a detrimental effect on the tsar, who had his cousin murdered in 1569, making an example out of him and signaling that anyone who dared to oppose him would meet the same fate. Then, he ordered the *oprichniki* to ravage the streets of Novgorod, which he suspected of harboring an anti-crown conspiracy.

But all these measures were not enough to reinstitute stability. Aside from being busy with the war in the north and west, Ivan the Terrible was also under constant threat from the south, where the Crimean Khanate frequently crossed the border and raided the Muscovite territories. By the 1580s, when Ivan was forced to admit defeat and sign peace treaties, his country had already entered a period of social, political, and economic decline. With all the resources directed to the army and the power stripped away from the local governments, Ivan was unable to keep the population in his vast territories content, as thousands had become impoverished. All of these factors had a negative impact on the tsar's mental and physical health, culminating in an accident in 1581 when he struck his own son in the head with a staff during an argument, shattering his skull and murdering him. Ivan spent the rest of his days being less and less involved in the country's politics before dying in March 1584. A promising reformer turned into a paranoid authoritarian, but history still remembers Ivan the Terrible as one of the final impactful tsars from the Rurikid dynasty.

The Time of Troubles

As one would expect, the death of Ivan the Terrible brought yet another catastrophic and chaotic period to Russia. Historians now fittingly call this period the Time of Troubles, and there is no clear consensus on when exactly it started or ended. However, one thing is clear: the effects of the Time of Troubles would be felt by the Russians for decades after the end of the period. The social and political consequences it produced require a rather in-depth analysis, as it brought about the emergence of the Romanov dynasty as the ruling family of Russia.

We shall start the analysis of the Time of Troubles right after Ivan the Terrible's death because the strength of the Russian state, which had been built up by the previous couple of generations, would start to dwindle quickly by the end of the 16th century. The person who succeeded Ivan the Terrible was his son Fyodor (also spelled as Feodor), who was a king with a rather different personality than his "terrible" father.

Fyodor had not really been interested in politics, preferring instead to spend his time reading religious texts and composing church music. Because of this, the institution that would be in charge of Russian affairs was the regency council, which was organized by the tsar and consisted of several major princes, his uncle, and, most importantly, a man by the name of Boris Godunov, the brother-in-law of the new tsar. One of the most important, as well as the earliest decisions, of the council was to exile Ivan the Terrible's youngest son, Dmitry, to Uglich as a precaution to avoid potential succession struggles. As we will see, this decision later proved to be very costly for Russia.

As for Boris Godunov, he quickly became the tsar's most trusted advisor and friend. By the late 1500s, Boris Godunov had made his name known, as he was a skilled diplomat and influential political figure, having gained the trust of the boyar council to engage in diplomatic matters with other countries. He personally traveled to the patriarch of Constantinople to ask for the independence of the Russian Church, which was still formally dependent on the Greek Orthodox Church, despite the latter's recent weakening due to the Ottoman destruction of Byzantium. Godunov's request was accepted, and in 1589, the metropolitan of Moscow, Iov (also known as Job), was elected as the first patriarch of the now-independent Russian Orthodox Church.

In addition to Godunov's diplomatic achievements, he also led the country to success on the battlefield throughout the 1590s, managing to reclaim some of the northern territories from Sweden and making an effort to end the Crimean Khanate's raids in the south. Then, he completed a peace deal with Poland to secure Russia's western flank before shifting his focus to internal affairs and leading the charge for new reforms to address peasant migration and fix some of the landowners' economic concerns. All in all, by the time Tsar Fyodor's reign came to an end in 1598, Boris Godunov had clearly become the most important person in all of Russia, sometimes being referred to as the "lord protector" in foreign records.

Tsar Fyodor had no heirs, leaving the country without a new tsar after his passing, which was a very difficult situation for any monarchy during medieval times. Fyodor would be the final Rurikid king to rule Russia after nearly seven hundred years of his family being on top. His death prompted Patriarch Iov to call a great council to discuss the succession. Boris Godunov would be the one to eventually earn the assembly's nomination to become the new tsar in February of 1598.

At first, Godunov declined the offer, but after seeing the overwhelming support from the assembly, he accepted. However, despite his illustrious status throughout all of Russia and Europe and his vast list of diplomatic and military achievements, a part of the Russian boyar nobility was reluctant to show their support. They feared Godunov would slowly try to reduce their influence in the country, so they challenged him, nominating their own candidate. Still, despite their best efforts, Boris Godunov was crowned as the new tsar of Russia in September 1598, swiftly dealing with the opposing boyars and starting a new era in Russian history.

Boris Godunov was an exceptional political figure, but even his might would not be enough to end the Time of Troubles. The series of unfortunate events started with historically disastrous harvests in Russia from 1601 to 1603, with thousands of lower-class people starving and being forced into poverty. The situation was so desperate that the Crown was forced to release the royal reserves and distribute food to the starving on a daily basis. However, this caused even more problems, as the poor flooded to the big cities to receive their portions but were still unable to get any food. In turn, they created bands and started assaulting others throughout the cities for supplies. Urban crime rates reached such high levels that city policemen were unable to deal with the newly formed bands, causing a special part of the army to be assembled and slaughter the criminals outside Moscow in late 1603.

The difficulties did not end there. Amidst the chaos caused by famine and crime, a person emerged who suddenly gained a lot of traction among the commoners, as they were desperate for someone to lead them out of their misery since Tsar Boris was not able to. This person would claim to be Prince Dmitry—the exiled son of Ivan IV—who had supposedly returned after the Crown's failed attempt to murder him in Uglich. In reality, the "Pretender Prince" or "False Dmitry," as many historians would later call him, was not Prince Dmitry. It was instead a former monk by the name of Grigory Otrepyev who had taken advantage of the Russian people's misery and decided to sweep in as the "hero" they needed. Since nobody had time to question the legitimacy of his claims, the starving people rallied around him. By 1604, False Dmitry went even as far as to visit Poland and Sweden to ask the local nobility for military and financial help. He promised that he had the potential to organize a full-blown rebellion and weaken Russia, which had emerged as the dominant actor in the region and had overshadowed their power thanks to the efforts of Boris Godunov. Thus, in the autumn of 1604, he managed to gain military support from a couple of smaller Polish nobles, assembling an army of about four thousand men, while the Swedish promised him gold to carry out his goals.

False Dmitry marched his men from Lviv to Moscow, being joined on his way by the upset populations of different villages, as well as many Cossacks who dwelt in Ukraine. The Cossacks were very interesting people. They were ethnically Russian but lived the horse-reliant nomadic lifestyle of the Mongols. As great warriors, they valued their freedom and wanted to exclude themselves from Russia to form their own separate state; joining False Dmitry was a logical move. After greatly bolstering his numbers, the Pretender Prince was able to overcome whatever resistance Boris Godunov was able to put up.

The morale of the Russian soldiers under the tsar was pretty low, as the famine had greatly affected their lives. After their defeat in January against False Dmitry's forces, they were completely routed, and the Pretender Prince secured free passage to Moscow. If that wasn't enough, Boris Godunov would pass away in April 1605, leaving the kingdom in the hands of his young son, who had neither the experience nor the ability to rule during such tough times. By the summer of the same year, he would be overthrown by the boyar nobles, who had held a grudge against Godunov for a long time, and False Dmitry was able to march into the streets of Moscow uncontested. Then, he summoned Queen Maria, the exiled mother of the actual Prince Dmitry, and forced her to publicly admit he was her real son. In July 1605, Grigory Otrepyev, the Pretender Prince, crowned himself as the new tsar of Russia.

Against all odds, Otrepyev had managed to become tsar. This was only the beginning of the Time of Troubles, as the new tsar found it increasingly difficult to maintain his position of power, something that stemmed from the fact he had only risen to power as an attractive figure during a time of turmoil. In reality, he did not know how to rule a realm, let alone such a vast kingdom experiencing difficult times. He never behaved like a royal, and those of noble descent quickly realized what had happened. To them, it was apparent False Dmitry was unfit to rule, even for a short period of time, as all he would do was throw feasts and spend his time with several different women. His rather lavish lifestyle was not meant for tsars, nor was it suited for an Orthodox monarch.

Otrepyev tried to make it up to the boyars by giving them back some of the privileges Ivan III and Ivan IV had taken away from them, but the boyars were no fools. Many of them knew that Otrepyev was an illegitimate king and only regarded him as a placeholder until a suitable replacement could be found or until the social problems could be better addressed. Because of this, none of them showed any real support toward the new tsar, despite his apparent display of gratitude toward them and despite the fact they had helped him overthrow Godunov's son.

Many other factors also contributed to the rapid end of False Dmitry's reign. For example, the Cossacks, whose help had been crucial for him to succeed in the rebellion, refused to answer his rule and demanded he step down from the position of tsar. After he refused, the Cossacks proceeded to ravage the Russian countryside and continued to be a thorn in the side of the Crown for years to come. The Russian people also quickly realized the fraudulent nature of the new tsar, as he failed to implement any sort of solutions to the problems they had faced for many years. They also disliked the fact False Dmitry was very friendly toward Poland, a historical rival of Russia. After all, his rebellion had largely succeeded due to the financial and military support from the lesser Polish nobility, and the tsar would be influenced by Western traditions and customs.

False Dmitry married Marina Mniszech, who was of Polish descent. She refused to have a wedding according to the Orthodox standards, as was the norm in Russia back then. Instead, she insisted the two get married according to Catholic tradition in the Kremlin cathedral in Moscow, a move that was considered to be utterly disrespectful toward the Russian Church and toward the people who had entrusted their support to False Dmitry.

In short, if the new tsar was not of royal descent, was incapable of ruling over his subjects, behaved incompetently, and acted disrespectfully, why should he remain in power?

The boyar nobility overthrew the Pretender Prince with relative ease. The boyars were upset with how things were going, and when the situation worsened at the beginning of the 17th century, the boyars instigated a rebellion and marched against the tsar. Led by Vasily Shuisky, the boyars took the Kremlin by storm but could not personally get to Otrepyev, as the latter attempted suicide and jumped out of a high window. His body was found by the citizens of Moscow and was mutilated to death before being burned. The ashes were shot out of a cannon. The reign of False Dmitry lasted for not even a year and saw one of the most gruesome endings to any tsar in the history of Russia.

The Struggle for Moscow

The Time of Troubles did not end with the boyar rebellion and the removal of False Dmitry. Vasily Shuisky replaced Otrepyev as the new tsar after being elected by a small group of rebels and Muscovites. People all around the country were content that the Pretender Prince was gone. Unlike Otrepyev, Shuisky was of noble descent and was much more competent than his predecessor when it came to almost every aspect of ruling. His reign lasted for the next four years, from 1606 to 1610, and Russia would sigh a breath of relief, at least compared to the previous decade.

One of the first things Shuisky—now Tsar Vasily IV of Russia—did was give the boyars even more rights to balance out their power in relation to the tsar. Shuisky understood he would need every bit of support he could for his reign to be at least somewhat longer than that of his predecessor, and he thought the boyars could provide that support. However, the main problem lay in the fact that not all of the Russian provinces were prepared to accept the newly elected tsar. The different principalities had largely operated on their own; Moscow did not effectively have control over them since the early 1600s. Technically, they still answered to the central government, but as Tsar Vasily's reign entered its first few months, many provinces rose up.

The tsar proceeded to deal with these rebellions one by one and was able to suppress most of them thanks to the rebels' lack of a competent army. Shuisky enjoyed the support of the nobles, who bolstered his ranks with professional troops. Eventually, however, Shuisky would face his biggest challenge in the form of a completely new insurrection in early 1607, which was led by a rather interesting figure by the name of Ivan Bolotnikov.

A slave-turned-Cossack before being captured by the Mongols, Bolotnikov had lived through a lifetime of struggle for freedom, something that inspired many from the Russian lower classes. He finally managed to escape from captivity to Poland, where he started gathering supporters for another rebellion against Tsar Vasily. Much like Otrepyev, he realized that it was the perfect time to seize the seat of the tsar for himself. Unlike False Dmitry, Bolotnikov did not rally the people around him just because of his "legitimate" claim over the throne. Instead, he was an inspirational figure for thousands of peasants, as he said that he was fighting for them.

Thus, with a force of about ten thousand peasants, Cossacks, and enemies of the tsar, he tried to wrestle the title away from Vasily Shuisky, marching toward Moscow in early 1607. However, as his movement grew in numbers, the fighters' spirit slowly diminished, and Tsar Vasily Shuisky was able to defeat the rebels in a head-to-head battle in the autumn of the same year.

Ironically, Bolotnikov's defeat sparked yet another rebellion—a sign that thousands were still upset with how things had unfolded. In one of the final insurrections of the Time of Troubles, another Prince Dmitry emerged. This man claimed to have been the son of Ivan IV and was thus a rightful heir to the throne. He had supposedly escaped murder both in Uglich and then in Moscow in 1606. Obviously, in the early 1600s, there was no effective way of spreading information, and a part of the angry mob quickly decided to side with the Second False Dmitry.

What made the matter even more absurd is the fact that the Polish wife of the First False Dmitry, Marina Mniszech, claimed the new man was her husband who had gone into hiding to escape the wrath of the boyars but had now returned to rescue the people of Russia once again. The new pretender gathered up his supporters in a small town named Tushino and organized a false government. Nicknamed "the thief" by Tsar Vasily's supporters, the new False Dmitry would challenge the tsar's rule in Tushino and its surroundings for the next two years, but he did not dare to march on Moscow.

Throughout the Second False Dmitry's rise as the leader of the new rebellion, Tsar Vasily Shuisky had been rather busy fighting off rebels in different parts of his kingdom and had exhausted his military. Thus, he approached the king of Sweden with a request to grant him a force of six thousand men in return for giving up claims of the contested lands of Livonia. The Swedish king granted him the men, which Tsar Vasily planned to use to crush the Second False Dmitry.

However, the news of the Swedish force under the Russian tsar was seen as a direct threat to the Polish king, Sigismund III, who decided to break the peace agreement between the two nations and declared war on Russia in 1609. Tsar Vasily Shuisky was put in a very difficult position, as he was not only losing support in the different Russian provinces but also had to deal with the rebellion of False Dmitry and the incoming Polish incursion.

Fortunately for the tsar, the Polish invasion shifted attention away from False Dmitry's rebellion. Supposedly, many of the Second False Dmitry's supporters dropped him, realizing the Polish threat was more severe. They united, in a weird way, for the defense of their country after trying to destroy their tsar for quite some time. As for the Second False Dmitry, he met a very gruesome death, being killed during an all-out brawl that broke out in his camp not long after Poland's declaration of war.

The Polish took the city of Smolensk in late 1609. Smolensk was a very important city, as it was perceived as a sort of gateway to Russia from the west. Its control was crucial for the kingdom's stability. The loss of Smolensk further weakened Vasily Shuisky's position, and he was eventually forced to abdicate since he was seen as unable to defend the country from a foreign invasion.

The popular assembly, which made the tsar abdicate and take monastic vows, tried to search for suitable alternatives, briefly giving the right to rule to a council of seven boyars. Amidst the crisis, the boyar council decided it would be best to invite a foreigner to become the new ruler of Russia, something that had happened many times in different European kingdoms in the medieval era. They chose Prince Wladyslaw of Poland, the eldest son of Sigismund III, to come to Moscow and become the new tsar.

However, Sigismund III did not approve of this. He was not amused by the thought of his son becoming the new tsar of Russia, as he had always desired to rule over Moscow himself. So, instead of stopping at Smolensk and being content with holding the territories that had historically been contested by Poland, he decided to march to Moscow. When the Russian people heard about Sigismund's advances toward the heart of the kingdom, they quickly realized they needed to settle their internal squabbles to unite against a common enemy. This was true for the vast majority of the population, including those who lived in the provinces. Soon enough, the Russians acknowledged the threat a potential unwanted foreign invader posed to Russia's integrity and banded together to avoid such a catastrophe, which was a rather uncharacteristic move if we consider the rest of medieval Russian history.

The people started organizing themselves into militia groups, which were all based in different provincial capitals. Since the kingdom was still without a king, local mobilization was needed at every possible location to fend off not only the Polish in the west but also the Swedish, who targeted Novgorod in the north, trying to capitalize on the chaos themselves. The militia groups gathered whatever resources they could find and quickly gained a lot of traction, even to the point that Patriarch Hermogenes gave them his blessing and endorsed their creation. Although they were not able to drive out the Polish from Moscow and its outskirts in 1611, the second national levy, which was assembled a couple of months later in Nizhny Novgorod, was able to reclaim the capital and give the Russians much-needed hope.

The Time of Troubles, though, was still not over, but it had entered its final stage.

Chapter Three – The First Romanovs

The first decade of the 17th century was perhaps the most difficult in medieval Russian history. The process that had started after the death of Ivan IV—searching for a suitable king to rule Russia—spiraled into years of uncertainty and chaos. Many claimed the title of tsar, but none were able to gain enough influence. As we observed, by the end of the 1610s, a foreign threat would unite the squabbling Russian people together to defend their country, and for the first time in a while, the future looked somewhat promising.

This chapter will explore the final stage of the Time of Troubles and talk about how domestic political maneuvering caused the Romanov dynasty to rise to the top.

The National Assembly's Decision

Thanks to the efforts of the national levies that had assembled in different Russian provinces to drive out the Polish from the capital, the situation had somewhat stabilized, at least compared to the chaos beforehand. However, after regaining control of Moscow, the Russian people were confronted with a very important question: who should be the next tsar? After the events of the past decade, it would be difficult to find someone with a legitimate claim to the throne. So, the matter was devoted to the newly formed Zemsky Sobor, a rather diverse group of about five hundred men from different provinces and social strata. Everyone was curious to see who would be nominated to ascend the throne.

The national assembly prioritized finding a person from a higher class, one accustomed to formal traditions and customs and who had a decent education and demonstrated personality traits that would be suitable for a monarch. The assembly started looking for a tsar when it first convened in June 1613 and nominated a couple of worthy candidates. Finally, after much consideration, it chose to elect a sixteen-year-old named Mikhail Romanov as the next tsar of Russia—a decision that would change the course of Russian history forever.

Young Mikhail was the son of Filaret Romanov, the Patriarch of Russia. When his son was elected as tsar, he was being held as a prisoner in Poland. Filaret had been promoted to the position of patriarch during the reigns of the False Dmitrys but had been part of a powerful boyar family before he was forced to take monastic vows under Boris Godunov. In the final decades of the 16th century, he served in the army and engaged in diplomatic relations with important states like the Holy Roman Empire, thus earning himself quite a reputation in Russia. In fact, during Boris Godunov's election, he was also considered a potential candidate but was overlooked, something that eventually resulted in Godunov forcing him and his wife to take monastic vows.

In short, Patriarch Filaret Romanov was a very important figure in Russian politics from the end of the 16th century, and the fact he was also the first cousin once removed of the last Rurikid, Tsar Fyodor, gave his son, Mikhail, a much better claim to the throne than others who were considered at the assembly.

Mikhail would officially be crowned as tsar in July 1613 on his seventeenth birthday. Although a new tsar was a significant step toward stabilization, the inexperienced Mikhail had a lot of immediate problems to address. The most important of these problems was, of course, the threat of foreigners to Russian lands. By the time of Mikhail's election, both Sweden and Poland had taken over vast chunks of land in the north and in the west, lands that needed to be liberated. Russia could not field an army that could compete in head-to-head combat against these European powers, as years of instability had completely destroyed the military.

The coronation of Mikhail Romanov.
https://commons.wikimedia.org/wiki/File:Vocation_of_Mikhail_Romanov_(Grigoriy_Ug ryumov).jpg

So, Mikhail decided to make peace with the two nations, and he was ready to compromise in return for more stability in his realm. In 1617, with the help of England as a mediator, Mikhail signed the Peace of Stolbovo, ending the war with Sweden. According to the terms of the treaty, he regained control of Russia's northern territories in Novgorod but was forced to give up claims in the Gulf of Finland. Still, it was a favorable agreement for the new tsar. This was followed by the Truce of Deulino with Poland in December of 1618, in which Russia ceded control of most of its western lands and surrendered Smolensk to the enemy.

The situation with Poland was much tenser than with Sweden, as King Sigismund refused to acknowledge the legitimacy of the newly elected tsar and still claimed the throne of Muscovy for himself. Although the terms of the truce between the two sides favored Poland because of the territorial gains, they also established a fifteen-year armistice, which was time the weaker Russia could use to build up its defenses and reemerge as a dominant actor in the region.

These diplomatic achievements went a long way in helping stabilize the situation domestically, as the Russian countryside was finally free from constant raids. The next important development would be the return of the tsar's father, Filaret, from Poland in 1619. Upon his arrival in Moscow, Filaret would not only regain the role of patriarch but also assume the title of Velikiy Gosudar ("great sovereign"), which was previously exclusively held only by the tsar. Filaret would essentially take over the control of the country after returning to Moscow, while Tsar Mikhail would follow the lead of his father until Filaret's death in 1633. Despite the fact that Filaret's assumption of power was highly unusual, it has to be said the reforms he implemented during his time were very effective, utilizing peacetime in a manner that would have long-term benefits for Russia.

Filaret was a person of strong character and had proven himself to the rest of the high-ranking boyars, securing the support the previous tsars had so desperately lacked. Among the new policies was, for example, the increase of funding for the agricultural sector. Agriculture had been the most important aspect of Russia's economy for all of its history, and boosting production was a great decision. In addition, a large portion of the Crown's lands, those that had been claimed by Ivan the Terrible as his own personal possession, were distributed to the servicemen. The reason behind this move was the fact that under the new owners, these lands would be given more attention and become much more profitable, increasing the wealth of not only the individual families that dwelt on them but also the state. New taxes ensured the investment the Crown had made into agriculture paid off dividends in the long term.

The state also forged favorable relations with several European nations, most importantly England, which loaned the Crown a considerable amount, which was much-needed support for a fairly empty royal treasury. The administrative sector was also a high priority. Filaret's and Mikhail's decisions were often supervised by the national assembly, which remained an important institution after the tsar's election. The balance between the monarch and the assembly was crucial for the successful implementation of new reforms, with the two often struggling to assume a more dominant role in decision-making.

Pre-Petrine Romanovs

Filaret passed away in 1633, a year after Russia and Poland had once again gone to war. Tsar Mikhail pushed for peace, as he believed the country was still not ready for an all-out conflict. Thanks to the diplomatic efforts of his father, the Holy Roman Empire brokered a peace agreement between the two sides in 1634. According to the terms of the "Eternal Peace," Poland remained in control of the western Russian lands, but King Wladyslaw officially gave up his claim to the Russian throne. This meant Mikhail's claim to the throne became even more legitimate, and his first years as the "true" king were given a much-needed boost. After the death of his father, who had undoubtedly overshadowed the inexperienced tsar since his return to Moscow, Tsar Mikhail ruled for about another ten years before passing away in 1645. Although the rule of the first Romanov tsar had unfolded under strange circumstances, Mikhail's reign was relatively successful and promised a prosperous future.

Mikhail would be succeeded by his sixteen-year-old son, Alexis. Tsar Alexis would become known as Tishayshiy ("the quietest" or "the most gentle"), as he was seen as being very intelligent, kind, and even-tempered. The new tsar, who was quite inexperienced and not really interested in politics, heavily relied on his court to rule. Boris Morozov, the tsar's mentor who was of noble descent, quickly assumed influence.

However, the first years of Tsar Alexis's rule proved to be very difficult, as the state, which was effectively under the orders of Morozov, tried to increase taxes after a universal census of 1646 determined the economic situation of the Russian population. Raised taxes and lowered salaries caused mass unrest, and corruption skyrocketed throughout the country. Two years later, in June 1648, people took to the streets in the capital, protesting the decisions of the Crown and forcing Tsar Alexis to completely change the ruling elite around him, including Morozov.

Prince Nikita Odoyevsky assumed most of the responsibilities previously held by Morozov, but unlike his predecessor, he was a more honorable and intelligent man. He greatly contributed to the legislative reform that came a year later, in 1649. The new legal code, the Sobornoye Ulozheniye, was drawn up. It touched upon the most important aspects of life for everyday citizens. It was much more favorable toward the middle class, which, as it was considered in the 17th century, was the backbone of the economy. The code reduced the power held by the clergy and the boyar nobility, limiting the former from acquiring more lands, while the latter was restricted when it came to peasant ownership. Middle-class merchants saw great benefits, as Archangel (Arkhangelsk), the city located in the northernmost part of the kingdom on the coast of the White Sea, was named the city where all foreign trade was to be concentrated—something most of them had wanted for a long time. The Sobornoye Ulozheniye was printed and distributed on a previously unseen scale; about two thousand copies were spread throughout the country to make sure everyone was familiar with the new laws. Although few could read, word spread quickly.

Despite these changes, the following decade was very unfortunate for Tsar Alexis. Multiple revolts occurred across the country, with Pskov and Novgorod protesting the new trade regulations, forcing the royal army to march to Pskov to resolve the issue with the help of the national assembly, which convened at the tsar's request. Four years later, in 1654, Russia suffered great losses due to the plague, which completely destroyed the Russian economy, as the workers were physically incapable of fulfilling their duties. This was also followed by mass inflation, as foreign trade deteriorated. The efforts to replace domestic currency with copper coins instead of silver proved to be catastrophic. After years of economic and social crises, the Crown was forced to stop issuing copper coins and release its silver reserves in 1663 since the decision had prompted many to rise up once again in protest.

Crises also erupted in the Russian Orthodox Church, which experienced a period of instability and chaos. The first main concern was a Russian Orthodox schism. Some prominent members of the church proposed new changes to the old rites and liturgical books to correct some of the "inaccuracies." They were, of course, opposed by those who believed that changing ancient, sacred texts and traditions were heresy, and they were prepared to stand by their claims even if it meant being excluded from the church. The ecclesiastical council that convened in 1654 addressed these issues and determined that new amendments would be added to the old texts, something that was confirmed a year later by the Greek Church as well as by the Great Moscow Synod in 1666. This did not undermine the protestors' spirit, as they chose to form their own sects despite the acceptance of new texts, causing them to be actively persecuted. They were sometimes referred to as the "Old Believers."

The second issue that concerned the Russian Church was caused by Metropolitan Nikon of Novgorod, who was elected as the patriarch of Russia in 1652. Tsar Alexis placed great trust in him and valued his advice very much, even granting him the title of "Great Sovereign" and making him as powerful as Patriarch Filaret had been about thirty years earlier. However, Patriarch Nikon was eventually blinded by the power entrusted to him by the tsar. He wished to establish the church's dominance over the state, causing him to be confronted by Tsar Alexis. Nikon would leave Moscow in 1658, feeling insulted and infuriated, although he refused to resign his see (Latin for "seat").

Over the next few years, the clergy was not sure whether to follow the patriarch since he had essentially become an enemy of the state. On different occasions, religious officials debated his status as a patriarch but could not reach a consensus that would please both their majority and the Crown. The matter would finally be resolved at the Great Moscow Synod in 1666, which was attended by representatives from Constantinople, Jerusalem, Alexandria, and Antioch, as well as powerful Russian nobles and members of the ruling class. The council decided to strip Nikon of his title and exiled him to the Ferapontov Monastery.

If economic, social, and religious problems were not enough, Tsar Alexis also had to endure a serious armed Cossack insurrection. The Cossacks, as mentioned previously, largely enjoyed their autonomy and were not exactly loyal to the tsar, at least to the same degree the different principalities were. Throughout the 17th century, they slowly migrated from their original territories of the Don River toward the east, contesting the Persians who held the lands near the Caspian Sea. Under an influential leader by the name of Stepan (Stenka) Razin, who had gained notoriety after his campaigns against Persia in 1668 and 1669, the Cossacks rose up against Moscow in 1670, demanding more equality and rights as second-class citizens. Razin's insurrection quickly gained traction among the peasants and lower classes and spread to include not only those living in the Volga Basin but also those who were generally against the tsar's rule. His army, which counted about ten thousand men, pillaged towns and villages on its way to Moscow, which was their final objective. Throughout the rebellion, Razin inspired thousands to rise up against the tsar and the cruel boyar nobles, who had mistreated their subjects for centuries.

In 1671, Tsar Alexis was able to muster up enough troops to crush the rebellion, thanks to help from thousands of foreign mercenaries whom he had hired to temporarily serve and defeat the Cossacks. The tsar was able to deal with the Cossacks in the most merciless of ways since they had been brutal when plundering and raiding the Russian settlements.

After his death in 1676, Tsar Alexis was succeeded by his son Fyodor, who was the eldest surviving son from the tsar's first wife. Tsar Fyodor III ruled for six years and was greatly influenced by the powerful individuals who surrounded him due to his poor health. Prince Vasily Golitsyn and boyars Ivan Yazykov and Alexei Likhachev basically took over the rule of the country, influencing the most important decisions and closely monitoring day-to-day affairs. In addition to some administrative reforms, which were aimed at taking care of the Crown's fiscal problems, they also took part in spreading some Western customs among the Russian nobility, such as the study of Latin and Catholicism. Under Tsar Fyodor, a new Greco-Latin-Slavonic academy was founded in Moscow, which was a great advancement in the field of education, providing poor children with much-needed access to high-quality teaching.

Unfortunately, Fyodor's reign was short-lived, and the tsar died without any heirs. He was succeeded by his brothers Ivan V and Peter, who ruled jointly. This marked the beginning of a new age in Russian history. The pre-Petrine period of Romanov Russia, a period that was instrumental for its political and social consequences and for successfully rallying the country from the devastating Time of Troubles, had ended. The pre-Petrine period certainly had its highs and lows, but as history would show, what was to come would be far more glorious.

Chapter Four – Peter the Great

Peter the Great is one of the most famous figures in Russian history. He is well known for his reforms, which influenced all aspects of Russian life, and is often considered to have been the person who modernized "old-fashioned" Russia, implementing a new European lifestyle and greatly contributing to Russia's struggle of finding an identity. He was undoubtedly one of the best Romanov rulers, so it is only fitting to devote a whole chapter to his reign.

Accession and Early Years

Peter ascended the throne of Muscovy under unnatural conditions. Due to the untimely death of childless Tsar Fyodor, who was Peter's older half-brother, the country spiraled into yet another succession crisis, but this time, the dispute was settled relatively easily compared to other instances in Russian history.

The point of contention was between the family of Tsar Alexis's first wife's side of the family (the Miloslavskys) and his second wife's side of the family (the Naryshkins). Peter, being the son of Tsar Alexis from his second wife, was supported by the Naryshkins, whereas his older half-brother, Ivan, was favored, naturally, by the Miloslavskys.

At first, the Naryshkins seized power, and the Zemsky Sobor— the great advisory assembly that had greatly transformed since Ivan IV had first called it in the 16th century—declared Peter as tsar. However, this did not last for long, as the Miloslavskys instigated a revolt to undermine the Naryshkins' power, attacking the Kremlin and killing a number of their rivals. Eventually, on May 26th, 1682, a day after the revolt, the two sides agreed to a compromise. Ivan and Peter were to co-rule, as senior and junior tsars, respectively. The great council also advised that before the two tsars could gain enough experience, real power should be held by Ivan's sister, Sophia, who thus became a regent queen (she was a pretty successful one too).

Queen Sophia contributed quite a bit to Russia's prosperous future, especially on the diplomatic and administrative fronts. In 1686, for example, she signed a treaty with Poland that gave Russia full possession of Kiev (spelled as Kyiv today). This resulted in the Crown deciding to pursue a policy of expansion in the south to gain better access to the Black Sea since it was a corridor to the rest of the world. The time was right since the situation in the Baltic was very tense. Prince Vasily Golitsyn, who acted as chief minister during Sophia's reign, aided the queen in many of her reforms.

Meanwhile, the junior tsar, Peter, lived in Preobrazhenskoe on the outskirts of Moscow, where he received his education. He became increasingly keen on warfare and military campaigns, something that influenced his reign once he became tsar. Since he spent his time outside of the Kremlin, he got to meet a lot of interesting people in his youth who would later become his most trusted friends, such as a Swiss man named Franz Lefort, who eventually was appointed as Peter's admiral and general. Perhaps no other person had more impact on young Peter than his teacher, Franz Timmerman, who was of Dutch origin. He taught the young tsar geometry and arithmetic. Timmerman was also the first one to take Peter to the port of Archangel, where Peter saw English and Dutch merchant ships for the first time. The city amazed him and made him fall in love with the sea and shipbuilding.

All these interactions with Westerners made Peter quite different from his predecessors, who, he believed, were devoid of the traits possessed by Europeans. Since adolescence, Peter regarded Europe as a symbol of freedom, knowledge, and progress, while Muscovy, corrupt as it was, stood for ignorance and the past. Peter learned how to speak several foreign languages, including German and Dutch, and regularly traveled to other countries to experience firsthand what it meant to be a European. All in all, young Peter had many passions and interests and possessed a worldview from the very beginning, which would make him different from almost every other Russian tsar before him.

A painting of Peter the Great.
https://commons.wikimedia.org/wiki/File;Jean-Marc_Nattier,_Pierre_Ier_(1717)_-002.jpg

Peter married Eudoxia Lopukhina in January 1689 and was of age to start thinking about a potential heir, a matter that was still up in the air due to the rushed nature of the joint tsardom.

Suspecting that Prince Golistyn and regent Queen Sophia were planning to conspire against him, Peter fled Preobrazhenskoe while his family, the Naryshkins, moved against the queen and her supporters. They managed to emerge victorious, exiling Golitsyn and forcing Sophia to take vows and join a convent outside Moscow. Under such circumstances, Peter and Ivan were able to rule without Sophia's interference in 1689. Still, Peter decided not to be fully involved with ruling the country and returned to his dwelling in Preobrazhenskoe. However, in seven years, Ivan tragically passed away due to ill health, meaning that Peter was now the sole tsar of Russia.

Military Reform

Peter the Great was, as his title might suggest, a great reformer, transforming every aspect of Russian life during his reign. Once he became the sole tsar in 1696, he was confronted with a long list of problems that required immediate attention. To the surprise of many, the young tsar was able to address everything, something that stemmed from his resilient and confident personality.

One of the most important matters was the question of the Russian military, which had become rather weak after decades of domestic troubles and foreign wars. It was apparent that it needed a top-to-bottom change, especially since Peter was at war from the day of his accession to the throne. The army was in rough shape at the time of his accession due to the ineffectiveness of old regiments that had become corrupt and pseudo-privileged. For example, the streltsy—the standing army that counted about twenty-two thousand men—were very old-fashioned and ill-equipped but still regularly paid and enjoyed their position as the tsar's "palace guard." The feudal cavalry, which was one of the oldest-standing regiments in Russia, was inefficient to maintain since it was composed of landowners who did not owe the king full-time service. Also, since the 1630s, some Western officers had been put in charge of special foreign units, which constituted the bulk of the army but were, in turn, very expensive.

Peter started to reorganize the army in late 1699, first touching upon the matters of conscription and volunteers. Volunteers were offered more pay and food to increase their motivation to join the army, and their numbers increased as the years passed, especially since Peter made a name for himself with his successful campaigns. In addition, according to new laws, landowners, the gentry, and the clergy were each to provide a foot soldier for a fixed number of households (for example, the clergy was supposed to raise one soldier for every twenty-five peasant households). The new recruits were not allowed to be serfs to ensure that crop production continued at the same rate, and they were also supposed to serve for life.

These new recruits were organized into different foot and cavalry regiments and underwent intense training to make sure they were always fit for battle. Peter also started retraining Russian officers to meet Western standards, something that increased the effectiveness of the army and laid the foundations for a more professional military tradition. Thousands of European muskets and handguns were purchased by Peter when he visited England in 1698, and their designs were copied and approved for manufacture in the coming years. New cannons were added to the army and the Russian fortresses to bolster defenses, and the personnel was retrained to man the new equipment. Even new uniforms, which were modeled after German ones, were commissioned.

All in all, the size and effectiveness of the military grew greatly during Peter's reign, and some estimates suggest that about 300,000 people served throughout his rule in the army, with well over 250,000 active personnel at its greatest extent. What made the army special was not only its sheer numbers but also the fact that Peter made sure they stayed up to date with new advancements in technology and strategy and were actively retrained every year.

One major aspect that also saw colossal improvements during Tsar Peter's reign was the Russian Navy. Peter's great love of shipbuilding would play a big part since Russia had never had a competent enough navy to challenge its rivals. Russian rulers of the past had never truly considered constructing a large naval force since it would require a lot of time and resources. Because of this, the tsardom lacked good shipbuilders, and the ships that were anchored in Russian ports were privately owned and of foreign origin. However, Peter realized that without a strong navy, Russia would be unable to take control of the Baltic and the Black Seas, which were the only two marine corridors available to Russia to access the rest of the world.

Several measures were taken to build up the fleet. Peter had gained quite a lot of knowledge from his travels and invited several experienced European shipbuilders to come and share their expertise. He commissioned the building of galleys and barges in the town of Voronezh. But to further increase the navy's size, he also ordered the landowners and the church to supply one ship per eight thousand households, just as he had done when it came to recruiting soldiers. As a result, the number of Russian ships grew almost exponentially during the first fifteen years of his reign. By 1725, records show the Russian Baltic fleet had become the largest in the region, counting about twenty-eight thousand active seamen, thirty-four large warships, fifteen frigates, and many galleys. This also meant the Crown spent heavily on maintenance; the navy cost more than a million rubles in 1724, compared to about eighty thousand rubles at the start of the 18th century.

To make sure the reforms Peter had implemented in the first few years of his reign stayed effective and that the army's and navy's progress would not be thwarted, the tsar also established several institutions that inspected the military. The Department of Military Affairs, the War Chancery, and the War College were all set up by 1719 to monitor the army's developments and make sure that problems were addressed quickly and competently. The naval academy of St. Petersburg, on the other hand, employed a lot of foreign marine officers and trained Russian sailors. In addition, many aspiring soldiers and sailors from Russia were sent to Europe to gain firsthand experience in their relevant fields and bring back valuable knowledge they could share with their compatriots. All in all, the advancements in the military remain one of the most effective measures taken by Peter the Great.

Russia at War

It is now logical to discuss how these military advancements shaped the wars Russia experienced during Peter the Great's reign. At the time of his accession, Russia had two main rivals: Sweden in the north, with whom the country had a history of conflict, and the Ottoman Empire to the south, which had reached the peak of its strength and had spread its influence to dominate the Black Sea. Gaining a significant advantage over these powers would bring great economic benefits and respect since the other European nations were watching the situation unfold. Since Peter wished Russia to become a true member of the European family, a decisive military victory was necessary.

Although Russia and the Ottomans had not gone to war with each other, they had warily eyed each other for a couple of decades by the time Peter became tsar. Neither one had a good enough justification to engage in an all-out conflict with the other, so it is unsurprising that Peter declared war on the Ottomans when an instance presented itself. The continuous raids of the Crimean Tatars on the southern Russian lands prompted Peter to launch a campaign against the Turkish fortress of Azov in 1695/1696. What is interesting is the fact that Tsar Peter would serve in the army as a bombardier sergeant, something that can only be attributed to his keenness regarding warfare and his personality.

The first attempts to successfully march against the Ottomans failed, as the inexperienced and still somewhat unprofessional Russian forces faced supply issues. However, this did not stop Peter from changing the army's command and making another attempt to capture the fortress. Peter increased the size of his army and commissioned the immediate construction of a navy in Voronezh, literally transporting ships overland from the heart of the kingdom to the south so the shipbuilders had a model to work with. He personally mobilized his forces and oversaw the construction of the fleet, which was the first navy he built during his reign, and set out to capture Azov once again.

By the end of July 1696, the Russians had managed to take Azov from the Ottomans, with Peter now serving as one of the galley captains. The victory at Azov was very important for securing a passage to the Black Sea and would prove to be useful in the future against the Ottomans. In fact, Peter's efforts against the Ottomans prompted him to start implementing many of the military reforms we discussed above in a quick manner.

What followed the Azov campaign was another of Peter's very intriguing decisions, as he decided to travel to different European countries to unite the Christian nations against the Ottoman Empire, which controlled most of southeastern Europe by the end of the 17th century. On paper, it was a diplomatic mission called the Grand Embassy to the West, but Peter also wanted to learn about Western traditions and technology and gather up military specialists to employ them in Russia. What made this one-and-a-half-year period so interesting was the fact Peter decided to disguise himself as Peter Mikhailovich. He refused to travel as the tsar, perhaps doing so to gain as many authentic experiences as possible.

From March 1697 to September 1698, Peter went from country to country. For example, he stayed in the Netherlands, where he studied shipbuilding in great detail from the best shipwrights in Amsterdam and also attended Leyden University in his free time to learn more about medicine, another one of his many hobbies. Then, Peter went to England, where he visited the dockyards in Portsmouth and Deptford, pursuing his passions and making contacts that would come in handy in the future.

As for the "official" purpose of his travels, the diplomatic aspect of the Grand Embassy was not as successful. The Ottoman problem had largely been resolved by the Europeans by the time of Peter's visit, and the Treaty of Karlowitz, which would be signed by Poland, Austria, Venice, and the Ottoman Empire in 1699, marked the end of Ottoman expansion into Europe. Although Peter was able to meet with several European leaders, these meetings never produced anything of actual political value. Thus, disappointed, Peter was forced to sign a thirty-year truce with the Ottoman Empire in June 1700.

In the first decade of the 1700s, Peter turned his attention to the north, where multiple European nations had allied together to end Swedish dominance in the region. Denmark, Brandenburg-Prussia, and Poland-Lithuania had all joined an anti-Swedish coalition and were more than glad to let Russia participate. Sweden had been facing some domestic problems, as the nobility was unsure about the newly assumed leadership of fourteen-year-old Charles XII. Peter declared war on Sweden in 1700 after having secured Russia's southern flank with the Turks with their thirty-year truce. He marched on the pivotal fortress in Narva on the Baltic with forty thousand troops.

However, despite Peter's seemingly advantageous position, the young Charles XII landed nearby with a force of eleven thousand men and routed Peter's army in October. The Swedish victory stemmed from their previous triumph against the Danes at Copenhagen, which raised their spirits and allowed them to pull off a small military miracle. The siege of Narva was abandoned, and the Russians suffered up to ten thousand casualties.

Narva was a disaster for Peter the Great, and the tsar took the following years to regroup. With Denmark defeated, Poland remained his only ally, so keeping the Polish king, Augustus II, on his side was crucial in achieving success against Sweden. Peter was very lucky the Swedish decided not to chase him after their victory at Narva, as they instead focused on slowly defeating the Poles.

While Charles was busy fighting Russia's allies, Peter launched another offensive in October 1702, this time successfully taking the fortress of Nöteborg, which he renamed Shlisselburg (Schlüsselburg in German) ("key fortress"). This was followed by several crucial victories on the Baltic coast, with the divided Russian army managing to take control of the poorly garrisoned cities one by one. By the end of 1703, it looked as if Peter had gained an advantage over the enemy, and for the next three years, the Russian army acquired even more territories in the region. However, King Charles of Sweden was able to retaliate quickly in 1706, defeating the Polish and forcing them to abandon the coalition. Peter was now left alone against an impending Swedish invasion, and with a long list of domestic problems as a result of the constant warfare and heavy taxation to finance the wars, he was put in a difficult situation.

Charles XII invaded in late 1707 with a large army of no more than forty thousand men. However, Peter was prepared. Anticipating the Swedish offensive, he retreated from the newly captured Baltic coast and razed everything to the ground on his way out. Moscow's fortifications had been upgraded, and Russia was ready to fight, for the first time in a long time, a defensive war. The Swedes were perhaps too confident due to their victory at Narva, as they thought the Russian army was inferior to them and believed they could swiftly defeat any resistance. At first, their belief was proven true. In July of 1708, Charles was able to confront and defeat the Russian forces at Golovchin with ten thousand fewer men (the Swedish had about thirteen thousand men, while the Russians had more than twenty-five thousand men). However, the Russians were able to put up a much better fight, inflicting many casualties and slowing down the Swedish king's advance. The Battle of Golovchin was a clear indication that Peter's military reforms had borne fruit, but it would not mark the demise of the Swedes.

Charles hoped his numbers would be reinforced by another force of twelve thousand under commander Adam Ludwig Lewenhaupt, but he had misjudged his ability to wage a prolonged war on foreign soil, especially considering the harsh conditions the armies had to endure. In fact, Lewenhaupt's army was intercepted and heavily defeated by Tsar Peter, so only half of the original force reached King Charles. And this half was demoralized and without sufficient supplies.

The scarcity of food and a harsh winter caused Charles to change his strategy. Instead of continuing toward Moscow, which he knew would be heavily defended, he marched south to Ukraine, where an anti-tsarist revolt was already ripe. Hoping to utilize the unpredictable Cossacks as allies, Charles spent the winter in Ukraine. However, Peter quickly reacted by reinforcing the southern provinces and sending General Alexander Menshikov to crush the Cossack uprising. Unfortunately for the Swedish king, the winter in Ukraine turned out to be the worst in a very long time, making the situation even worse for the invaders. In addition, the Cossacks were unwilling to offer their help due to their recent defeat by the Russians. So, in the spring of 1709, Charles XII and his forces, weakened by the winter and still experiencing serious supply issues, laid siege to the city of Poltava, northeast of the Dnieper River. This would turn out to be a fatal mistake.

Peter the Great arrived with his relief force in June. He was unable to assess the strength of the Swedes, so he offered to negotiate with Charles. The latter, however, refused and launched an attack in early July against Peter's army, which was about twice as large and much more fit for battle. After a four-hour battle, forty thousand Russians relatively easily defeated around twenty-two thousand Swedes in the Battle of Poltava, with both Charles and Peter narrowly escaping death in the midst of the flying bullets. The defeated Swedes were chased and routed two days later at the Dnieper. It was a decisive victory for Peter the Great and marked a turning point in the war.

Poltava put Tsar Peter and Russia back on the radar for other European powers. The word of his victory spread fast throughout other kingdoms, and it had the effect the tsar had desired for so long. It was also relieving for the people at home, as they had been upset with the new laws and expensive wars but came to rally for their victorious leader. As for the war with Sweden, it was clear that Russia had assumed a more favorable position, and Peter even convinced Denmark to reenter the war in 1710 after regaining Poland as an ally by supporting George Ludwig of Hanover to take power in a coup (the same man would become King George I of Britain). All of these developments earned Russia a much-deserved place in European politics.

With the confidence Peter had gained from his success against Sweden and with the relations between Russia and Turkey deteriorating since the peace agreement of 1700, it is not surprising that Peter went to war with the Ottomans again in March 1711, although it was actually the sultan who declared war, doing so six months earlier. Peter's strategy involved attacking the Turkish Balkan holdings, which was a predominantly Christian area. Although the Russians achieved some success at the beginning, attacking the provinces of Wallachia and Moldavia and prompting the Slavic peoples to rise up against the Ottomans, poor supply networks and overextension brought an early end to the war. Peter was forced to negotiate an unfavorable peace treaty, ceding back control of the fortress of Azov and much of the northern Black Sea coast in July 1711 with the Treaty of the Pruth.

Peter the Great would return to Russia for a short while after the peace agreement to marry his second wife, Catherine, in 1712 before embarking on yet another military campaign. This time, the Russians landed on the Finnish coast in May 1714, thanks to their newly formed Baltic fleet, and took the fight to the Swedish.

Peter had managed to hold onto the territories he had gained after the initial Baltic conquests, but since Sweden had refused to surrender after Poltava, he felt compelled to launch another offensive.

Two years later, Peter planned to launch a full-scale invasion of the Swedish mainland from Copenhagen with about fifty thousand troops but wisely called it off at the last minute, believing he was overreaching by relying on his allies to support him. For the next two years, Russia and Sweden entered a stand-off and even tried to negotiate a peace agreement. However, the terms presented by the Swedish in 1718 were so disliked by the tsar that he elected to withdraw from the talks, knowing he had an advantageous position, as he had heavily weakened the enemy and was still in control of the Baltic.

The Great Northern War—as the conflict has come to be known—finally ended in September 1721 with the Treaty of Nystad. The Swedes had failed to push back the Russians from Finland time and time again, and the Russian Baltic fleet had only grown in size and matured in experience. The Russian galleys were the masters of the Baltic, maneuvering in the tides thanks to their mobile and quick nature. This constant warfare and the threat of further invasion caused Sweden to reopen negotiations in November 1720, and this time, they made concessions Peter found favorable.

Russia gained total control of all the Baltic lands that were formerly led by Sweden, including Estonia and Livonia, as well as the part of Finland Russia had occupied since 1714. The Swedes, on the other hand, only settled for a payment of 1.5 million rubles and some trade rights in the ceded territories.

Peter the Great's Social, Administrative, and Economic Reforms

Let's now close out the chapter with what Peter the Great is perhaps best known for: his social, administrative, and economic reforms. It is worth noting that Peter was active in the process of heavily reforming Russia while he was busy with his military campaigns against Turkey and Sweden. Peter was not one of those kings who is only known for one particular thing, like success in war, for example. He had the ability to find solutions to many problems at once and introduced measures to effectively help Russia develop and Westernize, making him a great reformer.

Peter the Great was able to give the Russian economy new life, completely reimagining it and allowing the country to stay economically competitive with the rest of the European powers. During Peter's reign, Russia experienced a sort of industrial boom. It was not on the scale of what Europeans were able to achieve during the Industrial Revolution decades later, but it was enough to significantly increase the production of local goods and materials and encourage their export. Eighty-six new factories specializing in the production of textiles, iron, copper, sulfur, gunpowder, and weapons were built during his time as tsar. There was a tenfold increase in iron production, which Russia had in great abundance, thanks to its large size and diverse terrain. Metallurgy, on the whole, was greatly improved, mainly to meet the army's increased demands.

In the early 18th century, Russia controlled a large part of the economy, which, as a result, limited thousands of people from accumulating wealth. One of Peter's personal goals was to transfer the means of production to the hands of individuals, encouraging the creation of an "entrepreneur" class that would go into the business of manufacturing and would privately train laborers. Although Peter would not reach his goal, as most non-serf Russians relied on their serfs for income, the industrial reforms transformed the Russian economy, especially foreign exports. By 1726, about half of Russia's exports came from locally manufactured goods, and new factories and workplaces employed thousands of Russians who had suffered from unemployment before Peter's reign.

Peter believed existing administrative institutions also needed massive changes to make them more European and, therefore, more efficient and productive. Upon his accession to the throne, the power dynamics between the local institutions, as well as their exact roles and areas of governance, were unclear, so these problems had to be addressed too. Peter introduced changes that affected all aspects of the administration at once.

First, he established the Russian Senate to replace the Boyar Duma, a rather old institution that had lost its purpose and power when the Romanovs assumed power. Composed of nine (later, ten) members, the Senate acted as a governing body, overseeing the different provinces and tax collection. It was the country's highest legislative court, a function that was taken away in 1721. Attending Senate meetings was mandatory, and members missing any of the sessions would be at first fined and then risk imprisonment. This measure proved extremely effective, especially considering that only a third of the boyars actually showed up to the Duma meetings and wasted their time arguing over useless topics. Five hundred men were also given a new title (*fiskaly*) and they had the responsibility of being the eyes and ears of the Senate, rooting out corruption and fraud and making sure each officeholder fully completed their duties.

The creation of the Senate was followed up with the introduction of eleven new colleges, a system copied from Sweden. The colleges specialized in different aspects of social, political, and economic life and acted like modern ministries. The colleges of foreign affairs, war, and admiralty were the three most important ones and were created before 1718. The rest dealt with industry, commerce, finance, justice, provincial governments, and land ownership. Each institution had its own clear duties and objectives, as well as similar establishments and structures to each other, which made it easy for Peter and the Senate to regulate. The colleges were an improvement to the existing *prikazy*, which had mixed functions and goals.

Peter also tried to rethink the administrative division of Russia, something that meant more decentralization of power in the hopes of raising the effectiveness of governance. In December 1708, the Russian lands were redivided, this time into eight *gubernii* (governorships), which were, in turn, divided into fifty smaller provinces nine years later. The number of *gubernii* would eventually increase to twelve in 1718, and the system would last way beyond the reign of Peter. The main functions of these new administrative units were tax collection and recruitment, just like in other European countries. Peter personally appointed the governors for these territories, and they would directly report to the court. Peter also made sure that Ukraine, where the Cossacks were still largely autonomous, was under the firm control of the central government and introduced forced conscription and Russian laws. However, in the newly acquired Baltic territories, more autonomy was permitted.

To reach his goal of Westernizing Russian society, Peter knew he had to start with the members of the higher classes, as they held much more power than commoners. He forced them to look European by stripping them of their old, traditional Russian clothing and giving them Western attire. Peter even made the men shave their beards, which he believed were a symbol of the past and would be laughed at in Europe. The boyars were given new Western titles, like count and baron, and were forced to learn and live by Western etiquette. However, instead of weakening the boyars' influence, Peter made them more involved in politics, granting them different offices and making them army officials. He also introduced a new "table of ranks," a social mobility system that could allow someone to rise up to a higher hierarchy if they carried out their duties well.

Perhaps Peter's harshest reforms were those concerning the church, which the tsar thought enjoyed far more privileges than what was considered "modern" in Europe. The role of the church in 18th-century Russia was undeniable, but Peter was more concerned with the patriarch's status in relation to the monarch, as the two were often considered equals, with the former having just as much say in political decisions, thanks to his popularity from his supporters.

Peter made sure to push a radical church reform after the death of Patriarch Adrian in 1700, greatly reducing the number of lands and power held by the Russian Orthodox Church and forcing the institution to retrain and reeducate the majority of its clergy. The clergy was also deprived of tax privileges, and their spending was heavily reduced. To avoid joining the church as a means of dodging military service, he banned all men under the age of thirty from becoming priests. Finally, concluding his harsh changes, he set up a special spiritual *kollegiya* ("college" or "committee"), later renamed the Holy Synod, which made the church another one of the administrative units used for governance. By regulating legislation for religious officials, Peter asserted his dominance over the Russian Orthodox Church, making everyone realize the tsar was the most important figure in the country. The way in which he transformed the church remained for about two hundred more years.

Last but not least, perhaps nothing symbolizes the rule of Peter the Great as much as the construction of Russia's new capital, St. Petersburg, a clear symbol of the tsar's persistent nature and enthusiasm to bring the country closer to Europe. Built on the newly captured coast of the Baltic in flood-prone swamps, which made the construction extremely difficult, St. Petersburg was perceived by many as a dangerous and unnecessary project. Peter was motivated by his love for the sea and wished to leave Moscow—a city that symbolized Russia's old and backward ways—for something new, something that would be closer to Europe.

The workers faced many problems during its construction, and they were regularly forcibly transported to work under terrible conditions. Nevertheless, St. Petersburg quickly became the new center of Russia, thanks to the promotion and personal efforts of Tsar Peter. It would be the first Russian city that had a real urban plan, with buildings and streets modeled after what Peter had seen in Amsterdam and London. Peter would almost force Europeanness on its residents by requiring them to speak foreign languages and attend regular balls and parades. St. Petersburg meant a modern, Petrine Russia, and it remains one of Peter the Great's most remarkable achievements.

Peter's Legacy

It's not possible to include every single achievement and important occurrence of Peter the Great's reign simply due to the fact that so many events and laws require going into great detail to fully talk about their short- and long-term implications for Russia. However, it is undeniable that Peter the Great is one of the most widely known Russian monarchs of all time. He was arguably the most influential Romanov to ever ascend the throne of Russia.

Thanks to his efforts, Russia was able to reenter European politics and reemerge as an influential and powerful actor on the world stage. Peter's military, social, administrative, and economic reforms established a strong base for the country's future, and his transformation of Russian society and lifestyle, however radical and harsh it may have been at first perceived, prepared the country for its long and tumultuous future. Peter the Great had a long-lasting impact on his country and put great pressure on whoever would succeed him.

Chapter Five – The Age of Enlightened Despotism

Peter the Great singlehandedly started the process of Russia's transformation from a backward country to a modern, powerful empire of European standards. The next Romanovs would build upon those foundations to place Russia in an even more dominating position. This chapter will cover the Romanov dynasty right after Tsar Peter, mainly focusing on Queen Catherine II, the enlightened despot who is often credited with giving Russia a soul.

After Peter the Great

Peter the Great died in 1725; he was still relatively young, dying at the age of fifty-two. Historians believe that his persistent personality and always being fixated on overachieving on multiple fronts at once played a big role in his eventual demise. Peter also had a severe drinking problem, which, combined with the never-ending stress of running a country, greatly weakened his health. Since his health was slowly deteriorating, he issued a decree in 1722 that gave him the power to name the heir to the throne. Despite this, the matter of succession upon his death was still undecided. Peter had fourteen children throughout his two marriages, but most of them had died during infancy or at an early age, leaving Russia without a clear heir.

Thus, his widow, Catherine, was declared the first empress of Russia by a group of officials once Peter passed away. Catherine I would rule for the next two years. Although she had been a good wife to Peter, she had no real experience with politics and was not the person Russia needed, especially after such an influential period with Tsar Peter.

Peter's close friend, Alexander Menshikov, took over as the main decision-maker during Empress Catherine's reign and, despite being under constant pressure, was able to maintain the empress's authority over her subjects. After Catherine passed away in 1727, Menshikov and other powerful officials declared that eleven-year-old Peter would become the new tsar. He was the son of Peter the Great's son Tsarevich Alexis, who had died in 1718 after trying to rise up against his father's rule. However, in an unfortunate turn of events, Peter II died of smallpox before he could truly become tsar in 1730.

What followed next was a desperate attempt by the Supreme Privy Council, which played an advisory role during the succession crisis, to find the next suitable ruler. After some searching, the council chose Anna, Duchess of Courland, who was the daughter of Ivan V (the co-ruler of Peter once upon a time). Special terms were proposed to her that would divert the real power into the council's hands; the government would be something along the lines of a constitutional monarchy.

Although Anna accepted these conditions and arrived in Moscow as the new empress in early 1730, she proceeded to tear them up and dissolve the Supreme Privy Council, assuming more power than originally intended. However, much like Catherine, she was not interested in politics and instead formed a German advisory council led by her lover, Ernst Johann Biron, which took over the day-to-day tasks. Before her death in 1740, Russia took part in the War of the Polish Succession, where it managed to successfully support a pro-Russian king. Russia also fought in the Russo-Turkish War, where it defeated the Ottomans but gained very little.

Before Anna died, she named her successor: her niece's son, Ivan. She also said that Biron should act as regent before young Ivan came of age. However, soon after her death, anti-German sentiment became more widespread. Biron was ousted, and the empress's niece, Anna Leopoldovna, assumed power. This complicated matters even more, and the two sides, the former Empress Anna's German clique and Regent Anna's Russian supporters, clashed for power. A new contender emerged from the chaos. Her name was Elizabeth, the daughter of Peter the Great, whose safety was threatened by Anna Leopoldovna (at least, that was what many of her supporters argued). With the support of the French ambassador in Moscow and members of the court, Elizabeth successfully instigated a coup against Anna Leopoldovna and declared herself the new empress in 1741.

Elizabeth cared a bit more about politics and governance than her two predecessors, but she was mostly concerned with her love for lavish attire and was careful about who she surrounded herself with, making it very difficult for her to retain her popularity. Still, she would rule for the next twenty years, and her reign saw the introduction of several new important aspects. For example, the first academy of arts and the first university were both founded during Elizabeth I's rule. The Senate—an institution created by her father—also reemerged after being pushed aside by unofficial councils and advisory assemblies. Russia also succeeded geopolitically, winning wars against Sweden and Prussia during the Seven Years' War. It formed new relationships with Britain, Austria, and France and continued to gain prestige as one of the most powerful empires in the world.

Complications arose over Empress Elizabeth's successor. Upon becoming empress, she had no children, so she chose a presumptive heir: Peter, the son of Anna (the eldest daughter of Peter the Great) and Duke Charles Frederick of Holstein-Gottorp. Anna had been married to Duke Charles for many years now and had given birth to their son in Kiel. Young Peter, who was named heir presumptive, was thus more German than Russian and only arrived in Moscow in the autumn of 1742.

Interestingly, Charles XII of Sweden—Peter the Great's archnemesis—was also young Peter's great-uncle from his father's side. Upon his arrival in Moscow, he was proclaimed by the Swedish parliament as the presumptive heir to the Swedish throne. The parliament was not aware at that time that Peter had already converted to Orthodoxy in Moscow and was the heir presumptive to the throne of Russia. Thus, young Peter, who was still underage, had to renounce his claims to Sweden, even though those claims were very legitimate).

In 1745, Empress Elizabeth married Peter to her second cousin, Princess Sophie Friederike Augusta of Anhalt-Zerbst-Dornburg. Sophie arrived in Moscow, converted to Orthodoxy, and changed her name to Catherine. She eventually gave birth to two children: Paul, the future heir, and Anna.

Under these strange circumstances, Peter became the emperor of Russia after the death of his aunt, Empress Elizabeth, in 1762. Emperor Peter, now Peter III, was not really favored by the Russian nobility, as they did not really consider him Russian because of his German origins. In fact, one of the first decisions he made was to accept peace with Prussia in the Seven Years' War due to his personal fondness for Germany. For many years, Russia had pursued an anti-Prussian policy, and this decision greatly angered the Russian elite. Peter III even went as far as to make allies with the Prussians and ordered his twelve-thousand-strong army that occupied Berlin to march against the Austrians, his former allies.

Then, amidst all this chaos, he planned an invasion of Denmark to take back some of the lost lands of his duchy (remember that he was still the duke of Holstein-Gottorp). Peter even transferred about forty thousand troops to the Danish border in the town of Kolberg with the intention of starting a war with the Danish. However, before he could advance further with his plans, he was overthrown by his wife Catherine, which started a new era in Russian history.

Catherine the Great Becomes Empress

Catherine the Great, the enlightened despot, is another one of the most influential Russian rulers. Born as Sophie Friederike Augusta, Catherine was another German-born Russian monarch. Technically, Catherine was never meant to ascend the Russian throne and become empress, but the situation that developed after her marriage forced her to "save" Russia from her husband, whose foreign policy decisions were under great scrutiny from his contemporaries.

Unlike her husband, Catherine started adapting to Russian customs and ways of living upon her arrival in Russia. She enthusiastically learned the Russian language since, as she believed, a future queen must be well-spoken. In the early days of her marriage, Catherine became aware of Peter's dull and arrogant personality and started hating her husband, whom she thought was undeserving of being tsar. To entertain herself, she began reading books in French, something that would eventually become her passion. The writings of Voltaire and other contemporary French philosophers from the Age of the Enlightenment made the biggest impression on her.

As she drifted further and further away from Peter, whose presence she found unbearable, she started to get more and more involved with members of the court, often taking them as her lovers to answer the adulteries her husband committed. She became increasingly interested in politics and governance, and as the public's distrust of Peter grew, those with whom she had become acquainted through her openly lavish sex life started considering her as a potential replacement for Peter III.

The conspiracy against Peter would grow as the months passed, as he continued to make decisions that many believed went against Russian national interests. In comparison, Catherine seemed much wiser and cooler, somebody who actually cared for her and her country's future and who had enough knowledge, interest, and competence to become the next ruler of the country. Thus, in the summer of 1762, with the help of her lover, Grigory Orlov, Catherine was able to overthrow her husband and become the new empress of Russia.

Orlov, as well as many of Catherine's other lovers, would be involved in her court during the early years of her reign, with some of them having more influence than others. One useful thing that emerged from these connections was the fact that all of them were of noble descent, allowing them to forge a close relationship with the empress early on. It was an informal alliance, as the ruling elite favored Catherine, and Catherine favored the ruling elite. This relationship would be greatly reflected in some of the domestic policies she introduced.

Enlightened Despot

Catherine's rule is perhaps just as all-encompassing as that of Peter the Great, as developments were made in all fields of

Russian life, and both foreign and domestic situations got significant attention. Domestically, Empress Catherine had two main goals: to build upon and further advance the administrative and political foundations from the days of Peter the Great and to introduce a new educational reform that would begin the long process of properly reeducating all of Russia. Heavily influenced by the Western knowledge she had gathered in her early years after arriving in Moscow, Catherine wished to be the one who would start a sort of Russian Enlightenment. She believed the country desperately needed it.

Portrait of Catherine the Great.
https://commons.wikimedia.org/wiki/File:Profile_portrait_of_Catherine_II_by_Fedor_R okotov_(1763,_Tretyakov_gallery).jpg

Since the very beginning of her reign, she made an effort to expand the special schools in Moscow and St. Petersburg, namely the universities and military academies. These institutions were almost completely reorganized with the help of Ivan Betskoy, who served as the chief of the Imperial Academy of Arts and was one of the main advisors to the queen on educational matters. Together, Betskoy and Catherine implemented the first public school system in the country, as well as special schools for girls and orphans. This reform proved extremely successful; by the end of the 18th century, there were about 62,000 students enrolled in 550 different institutions. The majority of these students were in military and church schools, but the rest studied in newly-set-up schools. Catherine understood the importance of an educated middle class, so she made sure that many people had access to schools all around the country.

Providing education to the masses also complemented the spread of Enlightenment ideas through different means, like the translation and dissemination of popular Western works, not just in the highest societies of Moscow and St. Petersburg but also in other, more rural parts of the country. The creation of intellectual or literary spheres was greatly encouraged, and many new Russian writers emerged on the local scene. In short, it was a much-needed, effective cultural revolution on a never-before-seen scale. Unlike Peter the Great, who had tried to make Russia look and feel European, Catherine's efforts were directed at making Russia think like Europe.

When it came to administration, Catherine's reign saw a large increase in the number of officeholders and levels of bureaucracy. By the year 1775, there were about two thousand more state officials in administrative institutions with very high, desirable salaries. Interestingly, with the Charter of the Nobility, a decree the Crown issued in 1785, Catherine made it impossible for people of lower classes and incomes to be elected to office. This made it so the nobility dominated the civil service, receiving salaries in addition to their own incomes from their estates, exponentially increasing their wealth and power and, therefore, keenness toward the empress. This decision, which perhaps stemmed from her close relationship with the higher echelons of the Russian elite since her early days, raised efficiency when it came to administrative rule.

On the other hand, a new state council was set up in 1769 to act as an intermediary between the empress and the Senate, the latter of which got most of its functions back and was reorganized after a rather long time of inactivity. Despite this, the Senate never reached the same height of importance it had during Peter the Great's reign. In 1775, most of Peter's colleges were stripped of their functions. Only the colleges of foreign affairs, the admiralty, and the army were kept largely intact and became the most important administrative institutions in the country.

When it came to changing up the system of governance, Catherine's main goal was to combine some of the Western philosophers' concepts of the balance of power with German cameralism (the state's centralization of the economy to work toward the formation of a welfare state, whose benefits the subjects would enjoy). On this front, Catherine tried to separate the executive, legislative, and judicial powers from the institution of the monarchy as much as she could. But when it came to organizing self-sufficient effective middle and lower classes, which was instrumental for a cameralist society, she failed, deeming Russia unready for such a massive transformation.

Catherine the Great also introduced changes that would try to bring the Russian economic system closer to Europe, as the former had been lagging behind significantly. She encouraged foreign migration to Russian lands. Most notably, she welcomed German farmers, who settled in the Volga Valley and became known as the Volga Germans. The Volga Germans possessed modern agricultural technology and knew how to grow new crops that had been introduced to Europe from the New World, helping modernize Russian agriculture and boosting production. Ukraine and later the rest of Russia became well known for their wheat production. Thanks to the expansion of territories, Catherine was also able to grant many peasants new lands, which was a positive step toward increasing the wealth of the lower class and promoting production.

By revising and boosting local manufacturing, international trade flourished, and Russian exports reached the distant markets of the United States and East Asia, again thanks to the territorial gains Russia had acquired by the end of the 18th century. Textiles and metals were the most popular Russian goods, and some estimates suggest the total trade turnover to have quadrupled during Catherine the Great's reign. This contributed to the growth of Russia's ports, not only the one in St. Petersburg, which was the most important one by a large margin, but also the newly acquired ones on the Black Sea.

Financial reform followed, with the first banknotes and paper currency being issued in 1770. The country lacked silver, which it needed to finance wars. The overall economic growth produced more taxes for the state, which the state would often invest in different domestic or foreign projects.

Expansion during Catherine the Great

Not only did Catherine the Great's reign see some of the most influential cultural, political, and social reforms, but it was also characterized by Russia's rather effective territorial expansion and successful participation in different wars. More than 500,000 square kilometers of land were added to the country, including the pivotal regions of Crimea and the northern coast of the Black Sea, the Caucasus, and most of modern-day Eastern Europe.

Russia went to war with the Ottoman Empire once again in 1768 after the latter opened hostilities. The Ottomans were wary of Russia's potential expansion into Crimea or the Balkans now that the country had finally withdrawn from the Seven Years' War. In fact, Catherine had finalized the procedure of pulling Russia out of the war but retained friendly relations with Frederick II of Prussia, something that would come in handy down the line. Throughout the Russo-Turkish War, Catherine's objective was to finally get rid of the Crimean Tatars, who had dwelt on the northern coast of the Black Sea for centuries and who would continuously raid Russian settlements on the border. Catherine was able to defeat the Ottomans, most notably at the crucial naval encounter at Chesme and one of the largest land battles of the 18th century, the Battle of Kagul, where about 45,000 Russians were able to rout an Ottoman force of 150,000 and claim a heroic victory.

In 1774, with the Treaty of Kuchuk-Kainardzhi, Russia gained possession of parts of Crimea and gave Russian merchants free passage through the Turkish straits. More crucially, the Ottomans nominally said Russia was the protector of all the Orthodox subjects living in the empire. The victory against the Turks prompted Catherine to once and for all deal with the Crimean Khanate. Catherine eventually annexed the peninsula and destroyed the khanate in 1783, something that would lead to another war with the Ottomans in 1787. Russia would again emerge victorious five years later.

Catherine also saw success against another Muslim power: Persia. The two sides had their own interests in the extremely important region of the Caucasus, located between the Black and Caspian Seas. In 1783, Catherine managed to establish a protectorate over the Kingdom of Georgia, thanks to both nations being Orthodox Christians. She also pledged to stand behind the Georgians against any threat from the Persians, who had repeatedly invaded the small nation.

In 1796, Catherine was forced to declare war on Persia after it invaded Georgia and sent an army to expel the invading forces from the Caucasus. In the summer of the same year, the Russian army was able to defeat the Persian resistance, first in the northern Caucasus and then in modern-day Azerbaijan, taking the important cities of Baku and Ganja and forcing the enemy to retreat. Unfortunately, Catherine passed away before the conflict came to an end, and her successor, Paul, did not continue the offensive. He instead recalled the troops home.

In the west, Catherine the Great was able to restore Russia's status as a superpower, one whose interests should be taken into consideration during every major geopolitical event. Russia played an active role in the political processes of Central and Eastern Europe during the late 18th century. Russia was also actively involved in Poland's partitions (on all three occasions), something that underlines Russia's importance as a regional actor. Catherine had always recognized the significance of having her western flank secure and proceeded to place a pro-Russian, Stanislaus Augustus Poniatowski, one of her former lovers, on the Polish throne in 1764 before establishing a protectorate over the Polish-Lithuanian

Commonwealth in 1768.

This prompted the Polish nationalists to rise up in an insurrection. They declared war on Russia, which persisted until 1772. Catherine and her allies—Prussia and Austria—stood victorious. The three leaders of these victorious nations divided the conquered territories of the Polish-Lithuanian Commonwealth among themselves, stripping the state of about 30 percent of its bordering lands and significantly reducing its influence and power in the region. This was later followed by the Second and Third Partitions of Poland, where Russia, Prussia, and Austria continued to slowly whittle away the Polish lands until, in 1795, they completely annexed all of Poland-Lithuania. They then shared a three-way border in historical Poland.

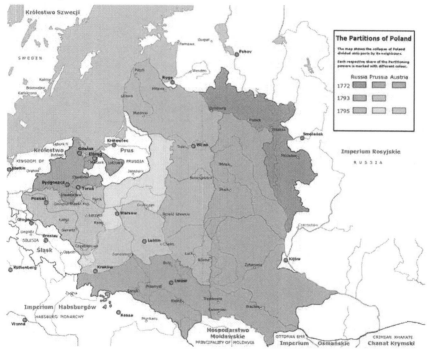

A map of the partitions of Poland.

Halibutt, CC BY-SA 3.0 <http://creativecommons.org/licenses/by-sa/3.0/>, via Wikimedia Commons; https://commons.wikimedia.org/wiki/File:Rzeczpospolita_Rozbiory_3.png

Catherine the Great was not a member of the Romanov dynasty by birth, being of German descent. Still, she remains one of the most prominent members of the ruling family of Russia, thanks to her distinct approach to ruling. Catherine's achievements were far-reaching, rivaled perhaps only by those of Peter the Great, so it is more than fitting that these two rulers deserve such a title. Due to Catherine's social and economic reforms, Russia was, for the first time, able to grasp what having a "European soul" meant. Rather than forcing Europeanness upon Russian society like Peter the Great, Catherine was able to significantly close the gap between Russia and the rest of the civilized Western world. Upon her death, one could see that Russia had become much more prosperous and glorious. It was a true empire.

Chapter Six – 19th-Century Romanovs

After Catherine the Great, the Romanov dynasty persisted for about another 120 years, but this period was in no way easy for the ruling family of Russia, nor for the country itself. Russia was confronted with many challenges during the 19th century (it is one of the most interesting periods in world history due to the many important political developments that took place during it). The Romanovs were forced to adapt to the new world order.

Paul I

The reign of Paul I, the son of Catherine the Great and Peter III, was the shortest of the Romanov monarchs after Empress Catherine. Paul replaced his mother after the latter's death in November 1796, and he was only emperor for five years before he fell victim to growing hostile sentiments, just like many of his predecessors.

In fact, Paul had never been on good terms with his mother, something that may be attributed to the fact that he was Catherine's first child with Peter. Perhaps resenting her child because of his relationship with his father, Catherine limited Paul's ability to engage in political matters, instead making him live at a private estate called Gatchina, which was outside of St. Petersburg. There, Paul lived with his second wife, Wilhelmina of Darmstadt (or Nataliya, which was her adopted Russian name), where he mostly devoted his time to reading Western literature and managing his estate. Paul even had his own small court, with whom he would discuss the potential implications of his mother's many policies. He also trained with the members of his personal army, much like Peter the Great had done when he was a child. However, it was clear that Paul was secluded from matters of real importance in St. Petersburg, and for that reason, he never managed to develop a good relationship with his mother.

Paul immediately replaced Catherine upon her death, perhaps fearing that Catherine would name Alexander, his eldest son, as heir, as he had been the queen's favorite. So, to avoid any further complications, one of the first things he made sure to do as emperor was to cancel the decree that said the monarch had the ability to name their successor, something that had been in place since Peter the Great. Instead, in 1797, he asserted the male line of the Romanovs would become the successor. All in all, it can be said that Paul was quite different than his mother, both in his policies and in the ways in which he implemented them. He was much stricter and often threatened those who opposed him in court with all sorts of punishments. His main domestic changes were directed toward suppressing the local elective governmental functions of the nobles, which, in turn, meant more centralization of power.

Paul's foreign policy was much more lackluster, and in the eyes of many historians, his failure to establish a strong foreign policy agenda eventually caused his doom in 1801. Coinciding with the rise of Napoleon, he chose to join the Second Coalition against the French emperor in 1796, which would end disastrously for the allied European nations and cause another coalition to be created in 1803. The failure of the Second Coalition resulted in Russia having unfavorable relations with its former allies, Britain and Austria, as well as with its enemy, France, which made Napoleon's defeat years later much more difficult. Although Paul formally annexed Georgia, which had been a protectorate of Russia since Catherine, he also planned a rather ambiguous and unnecessary invasion of India through Central Asia—a campaign that was the final straw the opposition needed to move against him.

In March 1801, before Paul could proceed with his unrealistic plans, a discontented group of high-ranking officials, including personnel from the military and the government, assassinated Emperor Paul in his chambers. The insurgents, led by St. Petersburg's governor, Peter von Pahlen, had gained the backing of the emperor's son, Alexander, and immediately declared him the new ruler upon Paul's death.

Alexander I: The Promising Emperor

Catherine the Great personally oversaw Alexander's education from a young age. The young Alexander did not live in Gatchina with his father Paul, instead residing with his grandmother, who put the future monarch in the hands of Frédéric-César de La Harpe, a Swiss national. He became one of the closest friends of Alexander and taught him a lot about contemporary politics, which was slowly being dominated by the revolutionary wave that followed the French Revolution. Alexander also received military education from Aleksey Arakcheev, his future minister of war and confidant, making it so that by the time of his accession at the age of twenty-three, he was quite familiar, in theory, with a monarch's duties and the political state of his country.

However, Alexander's reign coincided with a new era in Europe, an era of nationalism and republicanism, and the young tsar would be challenged by the problems that arose with it. Domestically, most of his time would be devoted to resolving the problems associated with imperial serfs. He would also feel the true wrath of Napoleon after his invasion of Russia in 1812.

At least when compared to his father, Paul, Alexander enjoyed much more sympathy from the Russians. Paul's tyrannical and vicious nature was replaced by Alexander's wise and more humane approach, and the young emperor was motivated to work toward making Russia better than it had been for the past five years. His liberal attitude prompted him to release those who had been taken without trial under Paul from exile and jail, a decision that made the public even more sympathetic toward him. Alexander also restored the right to write and publish freely and gave much of the privileges that had been taken from the nobles back to them.

Thanks to his Neglasny Komitet (private committee), which he formed with his most trusted friends to help work on new laws, he developed Russia's public education system. He provided new training facilities for aspiring teachers and built many schools and three new universities in the country. People holding a university degree had more opportunities to find jobs and start working in public office.

Despite acknowledging the fact that emancipating the serfs would help Russia modernize and catch up with its European neighbors, Alexander was much more reserved and opted not to go through with such a radical reform. During his reign, serfs constituted a large majority of the population, and by granting them freedom, Alexander risked his favorable position with the nobility, who provided the emperor with a lot of material and human resources. In hindsight, it was not the best of decisions, as Russia was forced to experience the age of industrialization and modernization much later than the rest of Europe. However, when we consider Alexander's personality and his unrealistic visions for the future of the backward country, which he had adopted from the theoretical concepts of the Enlightenment thinkers, it is not surprising that he refrained from pushing the reform.

The Man Who Defeated Napoleon

Instead, it is Alexander's achievements in foreign policy that really distinguished his reign. Upon his accession, he quickly tried to reverse the mistakes of his father by making Russia actively involved in European politics once again. He allied with Britain and got on good terms with both Prussia and Austria, the two nations he believed were instrumental if Europe hoped for a period of peace. Alexander also started to negotiate with France, but Napoleon Bonaparte, freshly crowned as emperor in 1804, redeclared war on the whole continent in hopes of achieving a total French hegemony and spreading the glorious revolutionary ideals of late-18th-century France.

Thus, in 1804, Russia formally joined the war against Napoleon as an ally of Britain but did not participate before late 1806, as Alexander was planning on waging war against the Ottomans to liberate the Turkish-held northwestern Orthodox territories (a war he did win after six years, in 1812). Alexander looked closely and planned his retaliation after Napoleon decimated Austria at the Battle of Austerlitz in 1805, forcing the Austrians to capitulate and exit the war. Napoleon also conquered Berlin and defeated the Prussians at the Battle of Jena-Auerstedt. Alexander's army would finally feel the wrath of the French at the Battle of Friedland in June 1807, where it suffered double the casualties of Napoleon's forces.

After the defeat at Friedland, Napoleon and Alexander met face to face, and the Russian tsar signed the Treaty of Tilsit, basically declaring that Russia would exit the war. Alexander was also forced to break off his alliance with Britain and join France's Continental System, an economic blockade that served to weaken the British. Napoleon, in turn, promised Russia would be free when it came to its disputes with Sweden and the Ottoman Empire. He also shared his overall vision with Alexander, which reportedly included the domination of most of the world by the two emperors. It was not the best outcome for Alexander, and the treaty would be received by the Russian public as humiliating.

However, the tsar did not plan to give up his struggle against Napoleon, and he sought revenge, not only for his own losses at Friedland but also for the defeats of his allies: Austria and Prussia. The two emperors grew increasingly friendly toward each other, and Napoleon considered Alexander to be his only friend in Europe. Napoleon even supported the Russians in a one-year war against Sweden in 1808/09, where Alexander gained control of Finland and forced Sweden to join the Continental System. It was a very interesting relationship, but Alexander knew it was doomed to fail, mainly due to Napoleon's ambitions of world domination.

Thus, after his defeat at Friedland, Alexander engaged in a rigorous military reform. Aided by his trusted friend Aleksei Arakcheev, the two aimed to strengthen Russia's main army, but military activity did not cease during this time. After Sweden was defeated in 1809, Alexander saw gradual progress against the Ottomans in Moldova. When it came to aiding Napoleon, Alexander refrained on a number of occasions, most importantly during France's war against Austria in 1809, respecting his old relations with the Austrians and refusing to send military help.

Alexander also showed his discontent when Napoleon invaded Prussia and annexed Oldenburg, which was the duchy of Alexander's brother-in-law. Alexander could not dissuade Napoleon from forming the Kingdom of Poland out of the newly acquired territories by the French Empire.

As a response and partially due to economic hardships that had come about due to no trade with Britain, Alexander started quietly smuggling goods to Britain and was eventually confronted by Napoleon. It was clear the relationship between the two sides, while cordial for a brief moment, was deteriorating once again. The conflict would reach its peak in 1812, when Napoleon, coming fresh from an array of victories against every major or minor European power, decided to launch a full-scale invasion of Russia.

Six hundred thousand French soldiers set foot upon Russian soil in late June 1812 with the intention of reaching Moscow by late autumn and forcing Russia to capitulate. Alexander knew Napoleon's army was far too strong to meet in an open battle and ordered his generals to avoid head-to-head confrontation as much as possible, instead luring the French deeper into Russia so the Russians could strike at an advantageous time. Alexander appointed General Mikhail Kutuzov as the commander of his armies, and thanks to the strategy the two of them devised together, he led the country through the Patriotic War, as it is called in Russia. During the great retreat, people evacuated major cities while the soldiers burned down everything that Napoleon could use.

An image of the French forces crossing the Nieman River, 1812.

The French emperor defeated the Russians, first at Smolensk and then at Borodino, by September of 1812, but he could not utilize the lands that had been made useless by the retreating Russian forces to his advantage. The French entered a deserted Moscow in mid-September and camped in the city for about a month. Napoleon found it difficult to continue his advance deeper into Russia. As Alexander had hoped, the French were soon forced to retreat, with Napoleon losing tens of thousands of men due to attrition and desertion. The harsh Russian winter had made it impossible for the French to use their superior numbers to their advantage, and Alexander had outsmarted his opponent, marking Napoleon's first major defeat.

After his triumph, Alexander urged the other European leaders to rise up and retaliate against the French. Prussia and Austria soon answered and entered a new coalition. Alexander led the coalition forces in a decisive battle against Napoleon at Leipzig in October 1813, liberating the conquered Europeans on his way west and heavily defeating the French. Then, he pursued the remnants of Napoleon's army, victoriously marching into Paris in March 1814 to cement his victory over Napoleon. Napoleon was forced to abdicate, and the Bourbons were reinstalled as the ruling family of France.

Alexander played a big role in the instrumental Vienna Congress, where the future of Europe was discussed by the victorious nations. Taking Poland as his prized possession, Alexander returned to Russia as one of the most successful leaders the country had seen in a long time. He was widely regarded as the most powerful monarch in Europe and continued to play a pivotal role in the geopolitical developments that shaped the continent for years to come. Just like his grandmother Catherine, Alexander was a new "arbiter of Europe," assuming a dominant position in European power politics.

After defeating Napoleon, Alexander would last about another decade on the throne, dying at the early age of forty-seven. His personality had always been unpredictable and easily influenced, something that showed especially after the tsar's return home from France. Over the course of the war, he had become overly religious and decided to blindly trust Christian traditions over the more liberal viewpoints he had adopted in his early years. Due to his new love of religion, he persuaded the leaders of Austria and Prussia to enter a "Holy Alliance," whose main aim was the promotion of Christian, conservative principles, which greatly influenced the development of republican nationalism in these countries. Alexander himself adopted rather conservative policies in Russia after Napoleon's defeat and further limited the rights of serfs, who had struggled for freedom for many decades. He also set up the so-called military colonies, distributing lands and peasants to his soldiers, perhaps as a reward for their resilience in the war. This policy did not yield any economic or social benefits whatsoever and created further difficulties for the serfs.

There is no denying Alexander I returned to Russia a completely different man, abandoning his idealistic and ambitious liberal views for conservatism, something that rapidly transformed into ruthless actions against the discontented populace. The Russians tried to rise up several times against the tsar, who became more tyrannical as the years passed. As more and more conspiratorial and secret societies emerged in the major cities to oppose Alexander, depression and paranoia took over, which had a grave effect on the tsar's health. After years of struggling with himself and his subjects, he finally met his end in December 1825 after visiting Crimea with his wife and contracting a severe disease, most likely pneumonia.

Nicholas I: The Classic Autocrat

As Alexander I had no heirs of his own, the throne was supposed to go to the heir presumptive, his younger brother, Constantine. However, Alexander's death brought about yet another, albeit this time brief, succession crisis.

Problems arose because Constantine, who never had much desire to rule, had married a Polish woman of common descent in 1820, five years before Alexander's death, and had thus renounced his claim to the throne of Russia. The next in line was the third brother, Nicholas, who was about seventeen years younger than Constantine and nineteen years younger than Alexander.

Alexander had actually chosen him as his successor after Constantine made his choice, but the process of Nicholas's coronation did not go smoothly. Those who had grown wary of Tsar Alexander in his later years saw his death as an opportunity. There were many high-ranking military officials and members of the upper classes who believed that Alexander had treated them unjustly by sending them off to his newly created colonies after the end of the war with Napoleon. The main goal of this brief but important uprising, which took place on December 26th, 1825 (December 14th in the Old Style Calendar and is known as the Decembrist uprising for that reason), was to convince the troops stationed in the capital to refuse to swear allegiance to Nicholas and to instead install Constantine. The rebels thought Constantine would help them take back the power that had been stripped away by Alexander. In the end, the Decembrists failed miserably, with those loyal to Nicholas quickly defeating them. Most of the rebels were exiled to Siberia or imprisoned during the trials.

Thus, Nicholas became the emperor of Russia. He was a very educated man in every field, including politics, and would quickly become one of the most conservative autocrats of the 19th century, reasserting the tsar's position as being superior to all bureaucratic or administrative institutions. Nicholas hated the concept of revolution and disloyalty toward the Crown, so he became an excellent embodiment of conservative, autocratic rule, which was slowly becoming old-fashioned in the rest of Europe. His contemporaries often remarked that he brought a sort of firmness and orderliness to his position that greatly resembled a seasoned army general.

And Nicholas was certainly experienced when it came to military matters, having been raised during the Napoleonic Wars. He was also a true royal, being engaged in high politics from a very young age. The best example of this is the fact that he married Princess Charlotte (Alexandra), the daughter of King Frederick William III of Prussia, and made sure the Russo-Prussian bond grew stronger than ever. His strict personality, which valued productivity, had developed after years of traveling in different European nations, of which England had made the biggest impression. In short, by the time Nicholas became emperor, he had almost all of the characteristics of a classic ruler; it was just a matter of how he would use them to benefit his country.

Emperor Nicholas I.

All of these influences played a big role when it came to the nature of Nicholas's reign. It can perhaps be best summarized by the official decree that was made in 1833 by the Russian minister of education, Sergei Uvarov. He proclaimed, on behalf of the king, the doctrine of "Official Nationality." The doctrine encapsulated three aspects that came to be the defining characteristics of Nicholas's rule: Orthodoxy (the holy source of the nation's morals and ethical conduct), autocracy (asserting the absolute dominance of the monarch), and nationality (an abstract concept of *narodnost,* which claimed the Russian people's ideal, traditional nature was characterized by their unwavering support of the monarchy and the royal family). Nicholas would force his subjects to live by these principles and would punish those who refused.

When it came to ruling, Tsar Nicholas I was very specific and demanding in his approach. He wished to personally be aware of everything that was going on in his vast empire and surrounded himself with ex-military members to enforce his strict attitude. He personally recruited all of his immediate subordinates, who acted as his personal assistants, and embedded them in all of the major administrative institutions.

Still, when it came to official meetings and ceremonies, Nicholas rarely showed up, thus diminishing the importance of many important structures set up by his predecessors, like the Senate or the state council. The emperor made sure his most trusted men, who embodied the emperor himself as if they were Nicholas's extensions, took care of the most vital matters in different parts of Russia and ensured productivity and maximum obedience. Nicholas believed he could maintain a strong grip on the country by doing this, though, due to his lack of initiative to implement actual changes that would affect the lives of millions of people, corruption reached high levels, with different state officials confused as to what their actual purpose was.

Nicholas I's biggest mistake undoubtedly was his refusal to liberate the serfs, as many European nations had already done. Fearing that it would result in a revolution that would topple the dominance of the royal family, as it had during the 1840s in other nations, Nicholas I further restricted the limited freedoms the serfs had. He was reluctant to adopt reforms that would grant society more liberties for that same reason. So, instead of trying to modernize the different social strata of Russia, he implemented different chanceries. The Third Department of the Chancery, for example, was essentially a personal police force, operating closely with the newly formed Gendarme Corps and making sure that every suspicious person was immediately dealt with. The Third Department's duties also included mass surveillance, enforcing censorship, and arresting criminals. Meanwhile, its leaders became very close to the emperor himself, who had grown increasingly wary of his potential opposition.

The final years of Nicholas I's rule saw the country dragged into the Crimean War, which would end disastrously for Russia. Now, Nicholas's foreign policy had never been strong, but he was generally on good terms with the more conservative European nations. Adamant about "protecting" the Orthodox subjects in the Ottoman Empire, Nicholas ordered his forces to occupy the province of Danubia, modern-day Romania, which was under Turkish rule, in June 1853. The Ottomans, with the support of the British and, later, the French, retaliated, declaring war in October and launching an offensive to get rid of the Russian forces in the province. Britain and France sent their fleets to the Black Sea to support the Ottomans (both countries had grown unfriendly with Russia, with Britain wanting a strong Ottoman Empire as a means of preserving the balance of power in Europe, while France had ongoing disputes with the Orthodox Church over the rights of Catholics in Ottoman-held Palestine).

All in all, the conflict was devastating from the very beginning for Nicholas, as the Anglo-Franco-Turkish alliance forced him to retreat his forces from Danubia. And if that was not enough, he had to deal with another offensive on the Crimean Peninsula, where the allies established a beachhead. By the end of autumn 1854, the French and the British had defeated the Russians at the Battles of Inkerman and Balaclava and had taken the crucial port of Sevastopol after a month-long siege.

It was all coming crashing down on the Russian tsar, who was quickly overcome by stress and paranoia and experienced severe health problems. By February 1855, his condition had reached the point of no return, and Nicholas I passed away. Some historians have suggested that he took his own life—an explanation that is not entirely unlikely, considering his distorted psychology and the toll of the Crimean War.

Nicholas I, who was a classic autocrat in every sense of the word, made many mistakes during his reign. He was reluctant to give up old traditions and encourage change in Russia. Who knows what would have happened had he loved Russia in a different manner. Would that have changed the way history would remember him?

Alexander II: The Liberator

The late Tsar Nicholas I was succeeded by his eldest son, thirty-six-year-old Alexander, who became Emperor Alexander II upon his accession to the throne. Alexander's reign would be much different than his father's rule, something that can be attributed to his early years, as the future heir had been educated by Vasily Zhukovsky, who possessed strong liberal and romantic views. Alexander had experienced the harsh autocratic rule of Nicholas firsthand and, due to the influence of Zhukovsky, had sort of become a liberal. Although Alexander was not as smart or hard-working as his father, he nevertheless realized the problems Russia was facing and decided to address them as soon as possible.

Alexander sued for peace in the Crimean War soon after becoming tsar, realizing the Russian military would not be able to defeat the combined forces of the Ottomans, French, and British. He preferred to accept defeat to buy more time to work on his domestic reforms to help Russia catch up with the rest of the European powers. Alexander signed the Treaty of Paris in March 1856 and was fortunate enough that he was not forced to give up any territories. Instead, the terms of the peace agreement forbade Russia from having warships in the Black Sea and also granted the disputed territories in Ottoman-held Romania a degree of autonomy. Christians throughout the Ottoman Empire gained more recognition. All in all, the aftermath of the Crimean War was not as disastrous as the military operations themselves, giving the new tsar a rather desirable outcome.

Once peace was established, Alexander started working on addressing some of the most immediate problems. One of the first reforms included the establishment of a brand-new railway system, which was very much needed in an empire as vast as Russia. Before Alexander, the only railway line connected Moscow to St. Petersburg. By the end of his reign, railways had been set up in most of the Russian provinces, amounting to more than twenty-two thousand kilometers (fourteen thousand miles) in total. The project of building a stable railway system was challenging, but it paid dividends, as it improved almost every aspect of Russian life. It helped with the flow of goods and labor, thus increasing trade effectiveness. It also helped with the transportation of the military in case war broke out once again.

The reform for which Alexander II is best known is his decision to finally abolish serfdom, freeing millions of people from essentially being slaves of landowners and giving them the opportunity to pursue independent lives and accumulate their own wealth. Despite opposition from the nobility, Alexander signed the Emancipation Act in 1861, which even included a decree about gradually granting the serfs small pieces of land so they could own something after they became free. Russia still lagged behind in overall industrialization and modernization when compared with Europe's best, but freeing the serfs was a massive step toward a more stable Russia and signaled the country was ready to abandon many of its old-fashioned standards. To the disappointment of the nobility, emancipation did not cause a severe economic crisis. Instead, it presented millions of people with new opportunities and is the reason Alexander II is often referred to as "the Liberator."

After the abolition of serfdom, Alexander reformed Russia's judicial system, which had essentially been in place unchanged for more than one hundred years. The new system was loosely remodeled and based on the one in France and was yet another step toward adhering to modern principles. Administrative changes included a subtle decentralization of power in 1864 in favor of locally elected assemblies, which came to increase the quality of life in the different provinces. Education was also revisited, and the government funded the construction of new schools all around the country, greatly increasing the literacy rate of its citizens, especially of newly freed serfs in the countryside.

In tandem with his minister of war, Dmitry Milyutin, Alexander reorganized the Russian military, which had shown its obvious flaws during the Crimean War. The two men focused not only on improving the training of regiments and introducing new technologies and strategies but also on making military education institutions significantly more effective. The military reform ended with the introduction of conscription in 1874, which was the "modern standard" of late-19th-century European militarism.

Alexander II was much more relaxed and tolerant when it came to minority groups, granting them different freedoms and rights. However, measures like releasing political prisoners from exile and imprisonment, recognizing Jewish and other religious minorities, and encouraging the creation of local institutions came to be a thorn in the tsar's side for the second half of his rule. As much as he had tried to liberalize Russia, Alexander had perhaps introduced a lot of important changes too quickly, something that inspired many to push for more freedoms in different ways, like organizing protests to gain more power or establishing secret societies where intellectuals would assemble to discuss ways of ending Alexander's conservative rule. Although he was much more liberal than his predecessor, Alexander was still an old-fashioned emperor in the eyes of many people, especially considering the fact that other European countries had slowly diminished the power of their ruling families.

Better education and more freedoms and rights to express their opinions caused the Russian youth to become increasingly anti-conservative, and members of the radical liberal opposition even tried to assassinate the tsar on a number of occasions during his reign. On the other hand, due to Alexander's more relaxed rule, the incorporated peoples, like the Poles, tried revolting on a number of occasions, forcing Alexander to brutally suppress their demands for freedom and an end to the monarchy. In a way, these developments made Alexander more conservative, pushing him away from his liberal views to protect his position as emperor. He made sure to reassert that the emperor was the single most important person in Russia, saying he had been granted his position from God, a characteristic thing that classic authoritarians say. It also had a great effect on his mental health, with Alexander becoming less communicative toward his family. He actually started an affair that would greatly influence his conduct over the next few years.

The late 1870s proved to be the most difficult for Alexander II, as the Orthodox Slavs in the Ottoman Empire increasingly started viewing him as their supreme protector, dragging Russia into another war with the Ottomans in 1877. Alexander had been reluctant to go to war but refused to leave the rebels on their own. The Balkan nations of Serbia, Montenegro, Romania, and Bulgaria, all of them supported by Tsar Alexander and mighty Russia, were able to defeat the Muslim Ottomans and largely drive them out of the Balkans. After one year of fighting, with the coalition pushing the Ottomans all the way to Constantinople, the Balkan nations sued for peace and achieved victory. Serbia, Montenegro, and Romania declared independence, while Bulgaria was established as a special autonomous region. In fact, Alexander is still revered in Sofia as the great liberator of Bulgarian people from the tyrannical Ottoman rule.

Despite Alexander's triumph in the war against the Ottomans, public sentiment at home had grown to be very anti-conservative. Secret terrorist societies that favored revolution had spread throughout all of the major Russian cities and posed a serious threat to the tsar and the monarchy's future. Alexander entrusted his interior minister, Mikhail Loris-Melikov, with the task of dealing with this problem, but the attempts to assassinate the emperor only grew. The terrorist groups tried everything to get rid of their monarch but were unsuccessful on multiple occasions. Finally, Alexander felt he had to give in, at least partially, to what the people wanted.

In January 1881, the Loris-Melikov Constitution was drawn up by his interior minister. The document would introduce two new constitutional bodies, allowing Russia to take its first step toward becoming a constitutional monarchy. However, the tsar was never able to officially issue the constitution, as he finally fell victim to assassins from the radical terrorist organization called People's Will. In March, on the same day the tsar approved the constitution, four assassins threw nitroglycerin and pyroxylin bombs at Alexander's closed carriage. The bombs mortally wounded the tsar.

Alexander III: The Peacemaker

Alexander II's second eldest son, also named Alexander, became the next emperor upon his father's death in 1881. Alexander III's older brother, Nicholas Alexandrovich, the heir presumptive, had tragically passed away in 1865, making him the next in line for the throne. Alexander III had been married to Princess Dagmar of Denmark since 1866, although the princess had initially been engaged to Nicholas (Alexander III's older brother) but was unable to go through with the marriage because of his death. Alexander III was the penultimate Romanov ruler of Russia and would rule until 1894. His reign would be completely different than that of his predecessor.

Deviating from his father's relaxed attitude and keenness of liberal thought, Alexander III made sure the monarchy retained its supreme power amidst the political turmoil of Europe. Being more than familiar with royal conduct and principles of law and administration, Alexander had, from a young age, developed a sense of distrust toward a representative structure of governance, firmly believing that it caused chaos and instability. Instead, he favored the traditional approach to rule, being heavily inspired by his grandfather, Nicholas I, and placing preference in the principles of autocracy, Orthodoxy, and *narodnost.*

Thus, Alexander had developed beliefs that clashed quite significantly with those of his father, and they would demonstrate themselves the most when it came to his change in the direction of foreign policy. In the late 19th century, Europe was quickly transforming geopolitically, and Alexander believed Russia had to keep up with the latest developments and assume its long-held position as the "arbiter of Europe." The most influential occurrences of the time included the Franco-Prussian War and the subsequent birth of a unified German state, the unification of Italy for the first time in centuries, thanks to the nationalistic movements, and the existence of a wavering conservative monarchy in Austria-Hungary.

Years of political maneuvering between these nations almost forced Alexander into an alliance with France in 1890 to balance against the Austro-Germanic partnership, which had been pushed by the new chancellor of Germany, Otto von Bismarck. This marked a deviation from the League of the Three Emperors, the previous alliance system between Austria, Germany, and Russia that had been agreed upon during Alexander II's reign due to his friendly attitude toward Bismarck. Although Alexander III's reign did not see Russia engage in any major wars, foreign policy developments played a crucial role when it came to establishing a new balance of power in Europe and, ultimately, became relevant at the beginning of World War I.

The League of the Three Emperors meets at Skierniewiece.
https://commons.wikimedia.org/wiki/File:The_League_of_the_Three_Emperors.png

When it came to domestic policies, Alexander would again transform the country's political landscape. He canceled the constitution his father had planned to officially issue and declared that his reforms would be directed toward revisiting some of the problematic characteristics of his father's reign. Alexander III firmly believed that restructuring Russia to include modern European principles harmed the country and his people. He instead promoted the revival of the three doctrines that had served the country for so long: autocracy, Orthodoxy, and *narodnost.*

Alexander III would start the process of Russification, enforcing the practice of one religion and speaking one language.

He also spread the idea that the Russian sense of nationality stood higher than that of other Europeans. For a diverse empire like Russia, which included a large number of people of different ethnicities, faiths, and nationalities, this seemed pretty problematic. The tsar completely diminished the importance of the autonomous structures established by his father by reducing their ability to have a say in major decisions.

During Alexander III's reign, Slavophiles—individuals who preached Russian and Orthodox superiority over their Western counterparts—enjoyed their most influential period. Alexander was a robust Slavophile in every sense of the word, and Russia would assume the role of the protector of all the Slavic Orthodox nations in the Balkans, which was yet another prerequisite for World War One.

Alexander III of Russia.
https://commons.wikimedia.org/wiki/File:Alexander_III_of_Russia_1892.jpg

All in all, Alexander III is referred to as "the Peacemaker" since Russia was not involved in any wars during his reign. His reign, in general, was rather uneventful, and while efforts were made to backtrack some of the liberal policies introduced by his father, Alexander III, as time would tell, was just trying to avoid the inevitable. Russia's conservative monarchy was outdated, and public sentiment had changed so much that a Slavophile emperor could not singlehandedly reverse it in his favor. Although some improvements were made when it came to infrastructure and technological advancements, mostly thanks to the generous funds that flowed into the country from its French alliance, Alexander III was unable to build on the liberal foundations his father had already created. He died of an illness in the Maly Palace in Crimea at the young age of forty-nine in November 1894, making his son, Nicholas, the new tsar of Russia.

Chapter Seven – Nicholas II, the Last Romanov

It is now time to take a look at the last tsar of Russia: Nicholas II Romanov. He ascended to the throne in 1894 after the death of his father and had to lead the country during one of the most difficult times in history. Although the Russian monarchy was already in a pretty rough state at the time of his coronation as tsar, few could have predicted the harsh ending the Romanovs would experience by 1917.

This chapter will explore Nicholas II's reign and talk about the most impactful events that transpired during his twenty-three-year rule, including the Russo-Japanese War, World War I, and the Russian Revolution. These major events are significant enough to be discussed on their own, so this book will only mention them in relation to the last Romanov tsar.

Accession of Nicholas II

Nicholas II was the eldest son of Alexander III, making him the heir apparent to the Russian throne. However, young Nicholas was neither particularly interested in ruling nor fit to become a tsar. He had mostly received a military education and, unlike his predecessors, lacked intellect and strength of character. This would prove problematic for Nicholas II, as his reserved personality was easily affected by the powerful people with whom he surrounded himself.

Although he deeply loved his wife, Alexandra, she possessed a much stronger nature and sense of resilience than her husband, which was difficult for the emperor to bear. Because Nicholas preferred spending time with his inner circle, Alexandra managed to quickly assert her dominance. Because of her, Nicholas's reign would be plagued by external influences, most importantly by Grigori Rasputin. Rasputin was introduced to the royal couple as a healer to help their ill son, but over time, he became heavily involved in Russian politics. He slowly climbed the ranks in Nicholas's court, thanks to his cunning nature. Rasputin gained the royal couple's trust before essentially becoming an unofficial ruler of Russia during World War One since Nicholas was often absent. Although Rasputin was eventually dealt with by those loyal to the tsar, the scandals that surrounded Rasputin had a great effect on Nicholas's reign.

The truth of the matter was Nicholas was deeply insecure and indecisive, which caused him to grow apart from the officials under him, whom he considered to be more experienced in governance and politics. In trying to uphold his position as tsar, Nicholas almost forcibly followed the principles of Orthodoxy, autocracy, and *narodnost* and severely punished those who had liberal tendencies and rose up against his rule. Local police forces became a tool for him to brutally repress "conspirators," the people who dared to go against his regime. All in all, one might argue his weak personality was the root cause of the many problems he faced over the years.

Nicholas II.
https://commons.wikimedia.org/wiki/File:Nicolas_II_de_russie.jpg

Nicholas II's indecisiveness would show when it came to both domestic and foreign policies, as he could not keep his focus on one particular aspect. Despite the ever-so-strong anti-royal public sentiment, he tried to further centralize the monarchy's power by limiting the agency of local political institutions. His contemporaries, including emissaries from the European countries, urged Nicholas to adopt more liberal policies, but the emperor never agreed with them.

He also could not decide where it was best for Russia to expand. During his father's reign, Russia had practically been declined the opportunity to have any colonies after the Berlin Conference, where the other European nations divided the world between them. This had a grave effect on the already insecure tsar, who believed Russia should maintain its influence on multiple bordering regions, including the Orthodox Balkans (which still regarded Russia as its sole protector), Central Asia, and, most importantly, Korea. The construction of the Trans-Siberian Railway signaled that Nicholas was ready to make an effort to increase Russia's power over Korea and to potentially gain access to its ports in the warm waters, which would not freeze come winter.

However, Nicholas II's interests clashed with those of Japan, another nation that was rapidly industrializing and growing its power in East Asia. After being unable to settle their disputes diplomatically, Nicholas was manipulated by his expansionist court to start a conflict with the Japanese over establishing a sphere of influence in Korea. The tensions reached new highs in early 1904 when the Japanese, who were also expansionists, suddenly attacked a Russian port in East Asia. By doing this, they declared war. The world watched closely as a mighty European nation engaged with a rising Asian power. Nations were curious about the outcome since a lot of new military technology was essentially being tested in the war.

To the surprise of many, Russia was heavily defeated, as its army was totally outclassed by the Japanese, who had made significant progress when it came to military innovations. Nicholas and his outdated and humiliated forces sued for peace and gave up Russian control of the province of Manchuria. Korea was quickly taken over by the Japanese by late 1905.

A quick defeat in a war against a weaker nation was the last thing Nicholas needed on his plate. The Russian public was outraged by the Russian military's humiliating showing. People took to the streets and demanded more freedoms, which they hoped would increase their quality of life. The tsar gave in, agreeing to set up a national assembly, the Russian Duma, and drew up a declaration that claimed no new laws would be implemented without the Duma's approval, essentially setting up a constitutional monarchy.

However, in classic autocratic fashion, Nicholas reversed these changes a year later in 1906 with the introduction of his infamous Fundamental Laws, which gave the sovereign complete control of the Duma. Nicholas could now act as the Duma when it was not in session or could even dissolve it if he so pleased. The Fundamental Laws also reasserted his position as the supreme commander of the Russian military forces and gave him immense powers to change the electoral system.

Instead of progress, Russia had taken another step backward.

World War One

In Russia, the 1910s was a period of instability and chaos. Nicholas blamed everyone but himself for his unsuccessful reign and replaced high-ranking officials often. He brutally repressed anyone who dared oppose him and still considered himself as being ordained by God. In reality, the influence of external personas on him would reach its peak. In short, Nicholas hoped for a breath of fresh air, as the duties of the monarch were making him experience stress and doubt.

An opportunity arose with the assassination of Austrian Archduke Franz Ferdinand in June 1914 by radical Serbian nationalists in Sarajevo. The assassination kicked off a series of events that would eventually culminate in World War One. Russia and all the major European powers were dragged into the conflict. Now, it is impossible to analyze the political complexities that were in place at the time of the archduke's assassination, but we will cover how Nicholas became involved in the war.

After the assassination of Franz Ferdinand, who was the heir to the Austro-Hungarian Empire, Austria-Hungary declared war on Serbia. At the time, Serbia was a small nation that had been struggling to maintain its independence from the conservative Austrians. Russia, as the traditional protector of all Orthodox Slavs, had guaranteed Serbian independence for quite some time and was thus forced to come to the aid of its ally when Austrian troops crossed the border and launched an offensive. But declaring war on Austria meant declaring war on Germany since the two were close allies. Fortunately for Nicholas, France joined the war on the side of Russia and Serbia, with the Great War kicking off in late July 1914.

Each belligerent had its own justifications and goals, including Russia. Although Nicholas tried his best to mediate the ensuing conflict between Austria and Serbia for about a month after the assassination of Franz Ferdinand, his court made him realize that the war was a sort of a blessing in disguise. If Russia could emerge victorious in a war against the great European nations, the people's trust in the monarchy would be restored, and the revolutionaries would be forced to give up their dreams of a revolution. It was now or never for Nicholas II Romanov.

Russia entered the war, hopeful that Austria and Germany would be defeated. Nicholas was confident the Central Powers could not withstand an attack on both fronts. And the Russians united behind the monarch and were ready to fight for the country's honor. However, soon enough, the truth was presented to Nicholas. The Russian military, which the tsar had refused to adequately mobilize during the July Crisis before the war broke out, was of no match to the Germans, who wielded superior technology and were familiar with new tactics.

The Russian army was undisciplined and lacked motivation. The only advantage Nicholas had was superior numbers, but it did not amount to much because of the use of trench warfare and the might of machine guns. Although the Russian offensive had made some progress against the German and Austrian forces, a quick response from the Germans, who had entered a stalemate in the west against the French and the British and were able to transfer the majority of their forces to the east, pushed Nicholas's troops back to their original front lines.

Back home, people grew more distrustful of Nicholas, as the tsar devoted all of his time, energy, and resources to the war effort and further neglected the already troubled populace. Influenced by his wife and stressed by the war, Nicholas replaced the commander of his forces and assumed total control himself, leaving St. Petersburg to go and fight on the front lines. This proved to be the final straw. The government deteriorated in the absence of the tsar, and Queen Alexandra and Rasputin essentially became absolute rulers. People took to the streets, and even those who were traditionally conservative disproved of Nicholas's actions. Many planned his murder in hopes of saving the royal family. However, it was all in vain.

The Last Tsar

Russia continued to slowly lose the war. Meanwhile, the tsar was not in the country, and the situation reached its absolute worst point by 1917. With new fronts opening with the Ottomans in the south and the Germans and Austrians pushing farther into Russian territories, the war effort seemed doomed for Nicholas, but he nevertheless continued to pour resources into the war to keep it going. Major Russian cities experienced constant protests organized by upset citizens. Most of these protests would last for a day or two and eventually fade out without a reaction from the government.

Crucially, on March 8th, 1917 (February 23rd in the Old Style), more than 100,000 factory workers took to the streets of St. Petersburg, demanding higher wages for the hours they had spent working in different industries for Nicholas's war. Joined by numerous female demonstrators celebrating Women's International Day, the people protested throughout the day, failing to get a reaction from the government. However, the strike did not die out the next day; instead, it became a general strike, growing to include nearly a third of St. Petersburg's workers, and it was slowly gaining more and more traction.

The demonstrators turned to violence, raiding different shops, police stations, and factories and overcoming the city police. The workers on strike protested largely against the monarchy, alerting the government, which was prompted to act to stop a full-on revolution from toppling the regime.

It was too late, though. The chain of command was confusing due to the absence of Nicholas and the Duma's inability to deal with the protesters. What became even more worrying for the tsar was the fact the Cossack police switched sides after seeing the magnitude of the protests. Instead of preventing further escalation, they joined the demonstrators.

Nicholas desperately ordered Officer Sergey Khabalov to return from the front lines to reinforce the city with a thousand men, but once Khabalov returned, his men also mutinied. They were tired of fighting a losing war and fed up with the high command's incompetence. They were soon followed by the Imperial Guard, who basically let the revolutionaries into the White Palace. By late February (early March in the New Style), it was clear the government could do no more. Nicholas had a revolution on his hands.

Bolshevik Red Guards at Vulkan Factory, St. Petersburg, October 1917.

The revolutionaries effectively took control of St. Petersburg and organized themselves into the Petrograd Soviet. They held their first plenary session in late February (or early March if you go by the New Style calendar), discussing the goals of the revolution and setting up committees to carry out different tasks. Then, the Soviet started discussing the possibility of setting up a provisional government with the Duma. During the negotiations, another rather valid question arose: what exactly was going to happen to Nicholas and the royal family? The revolutionaries were anti-monarchy, but the Duma mainly constituted of conservatives who supported the tsar. As for Nicholas, he resided in Pskov. The country was completely paralyzed, having likely realized the impending doom and awaiting the decision of the Soviet and the Duma.

Nicholas II was finally approached on March 1ˢᵗ (March 14ᵗʰ in the New Style) by the Duma representatives, who painted a clear picture of the situation to the tsar. They had come to the conclusion that the heads of the Petrograd Soviet, which represented the revolutionaries in the country, would be content if Nicholas gave the throne to his son, Alexei. Since Alexei had not yet come of age, Nicholas's brother, Michael, would serve as regent. What they essentially proposed to Nicholas was a constitutional monarchy, where the Romanovs would still be recognized as the ruling family but would lose most of their powers and instead play a symbolic role, with the country being controlled by other institutions.

Since Nicholas had no other choice, he abdicated the throne. He also declined the throne on behalf of his young son, as he did not want Alexei to go through the trouble of being the emperor one day. The onus was now on Michael to act. He was approached days later by the very same members of the Duma. However, instead of encouraging him to take the throne and become tsar, they convinced Michael to refuse it before the provisional government came up with a new constitution for the country.

Michael Romanov would never get the chance to formally accept the role, as the Petrograd Soviet and the far-left Bolshevik Party, which controlled Russia soon after the February Revolution, adopted an anti-Romanov policy. The Bolsheviks, who rallied behind their leader Vladimir Lenin, sent the royal family to the Tsarskoe Selo, an estate near St. Petersburg, effectively detaining them there for an indefinite time. Russia would tear itself apart, as the Bolsheviks fought with the Mensheviks, royalist "White Russians," for dominance of the country.

To keep the royal family away from the Mensheviks, they were sent to Ekaterinburg, where Nicholas Romanov, the last tsar of Russia, his wife Alexandra, his four daughters, and his one son would spend the rest of their days. In July 1918, as the Mensheviks tried to free the tsar from captivity, the guards watching over the royal family were ordered to shoot the family and their staff before burning their bodies and secretly burying their remains. It was the most gruesome death that could be imagined.

The guards were planning on a quick execution, as the family would be caught entirely unaware. However, the family believed they were going to be rescued any day now. They sewed jewels and other items into their garments for that very occasion. After the gunfire died down, all of the children were still alive. So, the guards shot, stabbed, and beat them until they finally died.

Although several imposters popped up as the years passed (most notably Anastasia), it has been proven that the entire Romanov family died that day. They buried the bodies in two separate graves. One grave was found in 1991; the other one, which contained the bodies of Maria and Alexei, was uncovered in 2007.

The Romanov dynasty had ended. Tsar Nicholas II, the final emperor of Russia, was defeated by the will of the people. Russia was no longer a monarchy.

Conclusion

The Romanovs are one of the most famous ruling families in European history. Succeeding the Rurikids as the main dynasty of Russia, they managed to stay in control of the country for about three hundred years and contributed greatly to its development. From Mikhail Romanov, who ascended the throne rather unexpectedly after the Time of Troubles, to Nicholas II, whose reign was cut short by the Russian Revolution, there is no denying the Romanov dynasty remains very influential, not only to historians but also to people who are simply curious about history.

Perhaps what makes the Romanovs so special is the fact that each of the tsars or empresses who came to rule Russia was different. They all possessed completely different personalities and strove to achieve different goals for the country's prosperity. Fundamentally, however, they all defined and embodied absolutism, albeit to varying degrees. The circumstances under which the Romanovs came to power in the first place explains this fact the best, as Russia, as a political entity, was much more diverse and complex than its European neighbors. The Romanovs mostly centered their rule around the principles of autocratic rule, Orthodoxy, and the importance of "Russianness" and thus were able to persevere during the hardest of times.

Peter the Great and Catherine the Great are undoubtedly the two Romanov rulers who are largely regarded to be the most successful. Thanks to their strong personas, they were able to maximize their power and lead Russia into a period of greatness and prosperity. That is why they are the only two who are referred to as "the Great." On the other hand, the last few Romanov rulers are considered to be weaker than their predecessors simply based on the fact they were unable to repeat or top the achievements of Peter and Catherine. What made the rule of those like Nicholas II extremely difficult were the unfortunate periods with which their reign coincided. The time of radical change in Europe did not favor the older, traditional system of the monarchy.

Still, it has to be said that the Romanovs did not deserve the abrupt and brutal end they received. Today, historians recognize many of the Romanov dynasty's pivotal contributions to Russian society. The Romanovs deserve their place as one of the most legendary ruling families in European history.

Here's another book by
Enthralling History that you might like

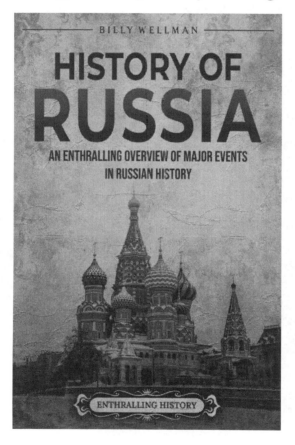

Free limited time bonus

Stop for a moment. We have a free bonus set up for you. The problem is this: we forget 90% of everything that we read after 7 days. Crazy fact, right? Here's the solution: we've created a printable, 1-page pdf summary for this book that you're reading now. All you have to do to get your free pdf summary is to go to the following website:

https://livetolearn.lpages.co/enthrallinghistory/

Once you do, it will be intuitive. Enjoy, and thank you!

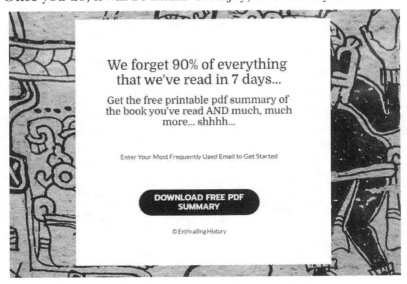

We forget 90% of everything
that we've read in 7 days...

Get the free printable pdf summary of
the book you've read AND much, much
more... shhhh...

Enter Your Most Frequently Used Email to Get Started

**DOWNLOAD FREE PDF
SUMMARY**

© Enthralling History

Sources

1. Bushkovitch, P. (2001). *Peter the Great: The Struggle for Power, 1671-1725* (Ser. New Studies in European History). Cambridge University Press.

2. Clements, B. E. (2012). *A History of Women in Russia: From Earliest Times to the Present.* Indiana University Press.

3. Dmytryshyn, B. (1991). *Medieval Russia: A Source Book, 850-1700* (3rd ed.). Holt, Rinehart and Winston.

4. Dukes, P. (1990). *A History of Russia: Medieval, Modern, Contemporary* (2nd ed.). Duke University Press.

5. DUNNING, C. (1995). "Crisis, Conjuncture, and the Causes of the Time of Troubles." *Harvard Ukrainian Studies, 19,* 97-119. http://www.jstor.org/stable/41036998.

6. Ellison, H. J. (1965). "Economic Modernization in Imperial Russia: Purposes and Achievements." *The Journal of Economic History, 25*(4), 523-540. http://www.jstor.org/stable/2116126.

7. Esthus, R. A. (1981). "Nicholas II and the Russo-Japanese War." *The Russian Review, 40*(4), 396-411. https://doi.org/10.2307/129919.

8. Heilbronner, H. (1961). "Alexander III and the Reform Plan of Loris-Melikov." *The Journal of Modern History, 33*(4), 384-397. http://www.jstor.org/stable/1877215.

9. Leontovitsch, V., & Solzhenitsyn Aleksandr Isaevich. (2012). *The History of Liberalism in Russia.* (P. Leontovitsch, Trans.) (Ser. Series in Russian and East European Studies). University of Pittsburgh Press.

10. Lewitter, L. R. (1958). "Peter the Great, Poland, and the Westernization of Russia." *Journal of the History of Ideas, 19*(4), 493–506. https://doi.org/10.2307/2707919.

11. Markevich, A., & Zhuravskaya, E. (2018). "The Economic Effects of the Abolition of Serfdom: Evidence from the Russian Empire." *The American Economic Review, 108*(4–5), 1074–1117. https://www.jstor.org/stable/26527998.

12. Meehan-Waters, B. (1975). "Catherine the Great and the Problem of Female Rule." *The Russian Review, 34*(3), 293–307. https://doi.org/10.2307/127976.

13. Okenfuss, M. J. (1997). "Catherine II's Restored Image and the Russian Economy in the Age of Catherine the Great." *Jahrbücher Für Geschichte Osteuropas, 45*(4), 521–525. http://www.jstor.org/stable/41049995.

14. PEREIRA, N. G. O. (1980). "Alexander II and the Decision to Emancipate the Russian Serfs, 1855-61." *Canadian Slavonic Papers / Revue Canadienne Des Slavistes, 22*(1), 99–115. http://www.jstor.org/stable/40867679.

15. Rieber, A. J. (1978). "Bureaucratic Politics in Imperial Russia." *Social Science History, 2*(4), 399–413. https://doi.org/10.2307/1171155.

16. Wortman, R. (2013). "Nicholas II and the Revolution of 1905." In *Russian Monarchy: Representation and Rule* (pp. 199–218). Academic Studies Press. https://doi.org/10.2307/j.ctt21h4wbq.14.

Made in the USA
Las Vegas, NV
11 December 2022

61892052R00061